Acknowledgement

Building *Zakery's Bridge* is a community effort. We'd like to say thank you to everyone who has contributed to this project. *Zakery's Bridge* began with storytelling. Our deepest gratitude goes to the children and families who shared their journeys with all of us. Many thanks to the photographers from all over the world who brought each page to life. Once we had stories and photos, our team at Shrieking Tree crafted them into the book, along with a web site and outreach materials. We cannot thank them enough for their artistry and dedication.

Beyond the pages, we continue to visit classrooms across Iowa where students experience workshops that go from reading to "living" these stories through art, music, writing, and other multicultural activities. Thank you to the many individuals, schools, and organizations making this possible. Our gratitude extends to CultureAll and Iowa's Council for International Understanding for their partnership and support. With them *Zakery's Bridge* is not only a book, it is a way to reach out into communities across Iowa, and beyond. Finally, we would like to thank you, our readers. For every copy of *Zakery's Bridge* that you purchase, you are contributing to literacy, learning, and the inspiration that comes from real-life stories shared from the heart.

Thank you!

Contents

ACKNOWLEDGEMENTS ii

FOREWORD v

AUTHORS' NOTE vii

ZAKERY'S BRIDGE 1

SUMMERS IN SAGAR 15

WHERE THE FLOWERS ARE 25

LITTLE DUTCH GIRL 41

DREMALI STREET 51

LEAVING LAOS 65

WHAT THIRTEEN MEANS 77

THE BEAUTIFUL ISLAND 87

PERRY LAS POSADAS 101

ABOUT CULTUREALL™ & ICIU 113

CREDITS 115

Foreword

BY GOVERNOR ROBERT D. RAY

Most people who come to Iowa cross a bridge to get here. Thousands of Iowans come from other lands and many, like the early pioneers, risked their lives to bridge the Missouri or Mississippi rivers on their journeys. They settled here to share the promise of what the Native Americans who lived here first called "Ioway," the Beautiful Land.

One of the most satisfying experiences of my service as Governor of Iowa was the opportunity to help people from all over the world cross what were often the most important bridges in their lives. Thousands of people left their homelands behind at one end of a bridge to cross to the other end with hope for a better life. That is why I am saddened when I see pictures of fallen or destroyed bridges, because it means life will likely be more difficult for those who need them. However, a bridge can be rebuilt, lifting spirits and restoring hope.

Such is the experience that awaits your reading of *Zakery's Bridge*. There is great insight to be gained in personal journeys as seen through the eyes of a child. These stories are of immigrant children who share with us both the pain and excitement of crossing their own bridges into an uncertain future. Some of these stories I have seen for myself while others I have learned, as will you, by being pulled along with an intuitive sense of hopes that will be fulfilled. So join hands with these extraordinary young people and walk together through these pages as they cross their bridges to their adopted land in Iowa.

Robert D. Ray

Governor Ray, goodwill mission to China and Thailand, 1979. (📷)

Authors' Note

BUILDING ZAKERY'S BRIDGE

Four years ago we set out to write stories of children's immigration journeys. As parents and writers we wanted to give our own kids and their peers a glimpse of what it's like to leave home and start over in a foreign country. After the first chapter we realized that writing this book was much more than listening to stories and writing them down. Each family brought its homeland to life in ways that went beyond storytelling. From throwing the colors of India's Holi festival, to breaking bread at the Eid-al-Fitr celebration that marks the end of Ramadan, we experienced our friends' cultural traditions firsthand. We had a lot of fun and learned much along the way—like how to properly eat keseda bread, and why it's better to arrive late to a Sudanese dance. We sang hymns in Spanish and "Happy Birthday" in Dutch. When we began our journey, we didn't know all of these things were happening right here in Iowa. Looking back, it is easy to see that each time we joined in a celebration, ate a new kind of food, or tried speaking a different language, we crossed a bridge of friendship and culture.

In *Zakery's Bridge* we hope that you discover something new and are inspired to cross "bridges" of your own—across Iowa, and across the world.

This book is dedicated to all immigrants
- past, present, and future - who bring their lives and their
stories to Iowa, making it a more beautiful place to live.

Zakery's Bridge

FROM BOSNIA & HERZEGOVINA TO IOWA

DES MOINES, IA

MOSTAR, BOSNIA & HERZEGOVINA

FACTS ABOUT BOSNIA & HERZEGOVINA

What is the capital city?	Sarajevo, population: 305,242
How far is it from Iowa?	5,201 miles
What is a favorite afternoon snack?	Cevapi (sausages wrapped in pita bread)
How many people are in the country?	3.8 Million
What are common names?	Girls: Zlata, Boys: Adi

If you have ever

traveled to a new place that seemed familiar or imagined being in a distant land, then you have something in common with Zakery Delilovic. For Zakery it is not an image of one particular place, but a gathering of stories about the country where his family once lived. In Bosnia and Herzegovina a city waits for him surrounded by mountains. Rivers run through with countless bridges connecting east and west. Mostar, the city of bridges, is a long way from Zakery's home in Iowa, but sometimes it feels like it's right in front of him. The first thing he sees when he walks in the door is a poster-sized photo of a stone bridge. Often he hurries past it on his way to school or soccer, but there are days when he is drawn to it—as if the old bridge is reaching out to him. Generations of his family have lived near the famous bridge, called Stari Most. Zakery's older sister and brother were born in Mostar, but for him it is a land yet to discover. It's hard to imagine leaving such a beautiful place, but that is what his family had to do to escape the Bosnian War.

I have seen Mostar in pictures, and my family tells me what it was like before the war. It's weird to think they lived in a whole other place before I was born. Sometimes I wonder what it would have been like if the Bosnian War never happened and we lived there. I dreamed of being in Mostar, and I couldn't believe it when my parents told me we were going! To see all of our relatives and the places they had told me about—not just pictures, but being there myself.

Leila and Haris, my sister and brother, loved the outdoor markets and splashing in the freezing Neretva River (📷). They played with kids from all different backgrounds. But when the war started everything changed. They had to leave. They could see fighting from their window. It scared them. My dad was taken away and they didn't know where he was. Mom,

Leila, and Haris stayed inside and got down on the floor whenever they heard shots. Everyone they knew tried to help each other, like the neighbors who hid them from soldiers. I can't imagine what that was like, hiding until someone could drive you to a safe place. At first my family didn't even know where they would go. It makes me feel sad they had to go through that, but I'm really happy they survived. Sometimes I think, 'Why did this happen in the first place?'

My mom says it's more important to learn from the war than to blame people. Before the Bosnian War split everything apart the Old Bridge was a symbol of peace. It was bombed on purpose. For ten years our relatives who live near the bridge saw it completely ruined. Then, with a lot of help, they brought the original boulders back up from the river bottom and started rebuilding.

A Bustling Bosnian Market in Sarajevo

A Building Bombed in the War

The Bosnian War

The Bosnian War took place from 1992 to 1995. Forces from nearby Serbia and Croatia fought to control Bosnia and Herzegovina, where Zakery's family lived.

My aunts and uncles were so happy when the bridge was finished. They couldn't believe that people would rebuild it for them. It took a long time to put all the stones back together. I remember hearing about the celebration when the bridge re-opened. I couldn't wait to see it and finally meet my relatives. In some ways Bosnia seemed familiar, and in some ways it was like a foreign country.

I don't speak Bosnian as well as the rest of my family, but I try. Talking with my relatives on the phone helps me keep in touch and practice the language. I talk with my cousin, Adi, who is a year older than me. We both love soccer and video games. Before we left for our trip I really practiced speaking Bosnian.
At school I taught my class a few words:

Zdravo (zdRAH-vo) means "hello."
Sta Radis (shta-RAD-ish) is "how are you doing?"
Sta ima (shta-EE-mah) is like, "what's up?"
It literally means "where are you?"
Suti (SHU-tee) means "be quiet!"

I told one of my teachers how to say "suti" to get the kids' attention and it worked. Most of my friends liked learning about Bosnia and Herzegovina. Like the time I sang the song "There Is a Beautiful Girl" in Bosnian for my class. But sometimes kids made fun of it, or they didn't understand. One kid kept saying 'Bosnia doesn't exist. It's just a fantasy.' It made me mad. My teacher asked me to show the class some things from Mostar. I brought a book to school with Bosnian stories, written in the language to show that it does exist.

The Old Bridge, or Stari Most, was built in 1566 and was the largest single stone span bridge in the world. Workers cemented limestone boulders together with a mixture of eggs, flour, horsehair, and milk. For centuries it was thought to be indestructible.

Bridge Blueprints

In 1993, during the Bosnian War, the Old Bridge was bombed. Its centuries-old stones plunged to the bottom of the Neretva River. With cooperation from around the world, the bridge reopened in 2004. People from both sides of Mostar gathered to celebrate this symbol of peace.

Bosnia and Herzegovina

It sounds like two names, but Bosnia and Herzegovina is the official name of the country where Zakery's family began. At one time, Bosnia and Herzegovina were two separate territories, but they have been linked together since the 1400's. Bosnia is the larger northern area and Herzegovina is the smaller, southwestern part surrounding Mostar. Although many people shorten the name to Bosnia, the Delilovic's honor their homeland by using the country's full name.

BOSNIA

MOSTAR

HERZEGOVINA

A Map to Zakery's Bridge

Just look at all the words in this book! (📷) Most of the class thought it was cool to see a book in another language. Mrs. Keese helped me show the class how important Bosnia and Herzegovina is. She made me feel proud about sharing my language and where my family is from.

It's important for me to know about Bosnia and Herzegovina. When I'm a dad, the best thing for me to pass on to my kids is the language—for them to know where we came from. These are things that we take with us wherever we go in the world.

Mom, Dad, Leila, and Haris had to leave everything behind—house, toys, everything. Sometimes, if I hear my friends complaining because they didn't get the PlayStation or a game they wanted, I think 'a PlayStation is nothing compared to a house. A video game is not that big of a deal.' And I want to ask them, 'What would you take if you could only grab a few things and you weren't coming back?'

When Zakery crossed

the Old Bridge a new chapter in his life unfolded. (📷) He stood in the center of the bridge looking over the Neretva River, which seemed greener and wider than he had imagined. After eleven years, he met his relatives and visited places he had seen in pictures. Mostar means keeper of the bridge. In many ways Zakery's family and the people who live here are not only keepers of a bridge but keepers of peace. Reconstructing the Old Bridge did more than put stones back in place. It reunited families like Zakery's and strengthened the peace-building process.

Daring Divers

The skakaci [ska-KACH-ee] are skilled divers who brave cold water and dangerous heights when they jump, head-first, from the Old Bridge in Mostar.

The stone arch is 20 meters, (65 feet, 7 inches), from the river below. Divers have come from all over Europe to compete. The tradition of diving into the Neretva River began centuries ago after the bridge was originally built.

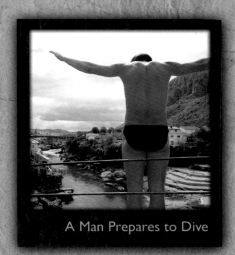

A Man Prepares to Dive

Going to Mostar was the best time in my life. When I met all of my relatives, they hugged me, and kissed me, and embarrassed me . . . My grandmother was so happy she was crying.

When I first saw my cousin, Adi, I was surprised—he looked like me! Everyone kept saying how much we looked alike. Our parents were talking and talking in Bosnian. I stayed at Adi's house for most of our trip. Some nights we hung out, playing cards and eating chips. Our video games were in different languages. (📷) He thought it was cool that I taught him English words. By the

time we left I was speaking almost all Bosnian.

Walking across the bridge for the first time was even better than I had imagined. The river is a very, very beautiful place. The water is green. There's cobbles on the bridge and roses growing along the side. Even the air is nice. Houses and buildings are made from the same stone as the bridge, with orange roofs. We watched the famous divers that my dad had always told me about. They're called skakaci, [ska-KACH-ee] and they dive from the very top of the bridge to see who is best. It's a long ways down and the water is freezing cold. Everyone was saying, 'Look at the guy jumping off the bridge!' They yelled, 'Zagnjuri!' [zan-JUR-ee] which means 'dive!' Most people don't dive like that, only really brave people. They go in for a minute and then they have to get out. People run to see the divers and some threw money for them.

Across the bridge was a sign on one of the rocks that said: 'Never Forget'. . .So many people died or had to leave because of the Bosnian War, they don't want anyone to forget what happened.

We drove to the house where my dad lived when he was little. Now my cousin, Janita, and her parents live there. From a distance it looked like the other stone houses, but when we got closer we could see the damage. The part where Janita lives is okay, but the other half was destroyed in the war. The wall is there, two rooms and the kitchen, but the next room is gone.

Signs of War

The Bosnian War ended in 1995 but it has been a slow recovery for this war-torn region. In Mostar there are roads, homes, and buildings with scars of destruction, and people who do not have the jobs they had before the war. For Zakery, the greatest proof of the War was outside of Mostar where his cousin, Janita, lives.

Vedran Smailović Plays a Cello in the broken National Library

2003 Bridge Reconstruction

Uncle Rutko put the stones back so it looked like the wall had been moved. My dad told me their father built that house. It was sad to see it like that. It would take a lot of money to make it the way it was. If I have money, one day when I grow up, maybe I could go back there and fix it.

I was so happy to see Janita, Aunt Zijada, and Uncle Rutko. I brought Janita a Barbie with a little remote control car. She was jumping up and down she was so excited. We played tag, and games, and rode bikes on the curving streets. There were lots of cracks in the road and more buildings and houses that have never been fixed. But for Janita it has always been like this. We rode bikes until we found her school. I taught her 'thank you' in English and some numbers and ABC's. I wish they could come to America and find a job for Uncle Rutko, but it is hard to have enough money to come. Janita and I were having so much fun we didn't want to leave her house, but we all had dinner in Mostar.

We sat outside under a bridge. It was amazing, with waterfalls and lights on the river. The current sounded like little waves. There was live music and people singing Bosnian songs. They were so nice. They asked me if I wanted to sing. So I said 'yeah, sure.' I sang "There Is a Beautiful Girl" in Bosnian right up front with the microphone. Everyone clapped, and it was pretty cool. I was a little nervous, but I remembered all the words.

Another cool thing along the river are the outdoor markets. Everything is hand-made out of leather—coats, purses, necklaces, slippers. We bought presents for my sister and brother, and I got a pair of slippers to take back and a bronze model of the Old Bridge.

We went to my mom's old neighborhood, and I met Uncle Edin and Uncle Emir, her brothers. They asked about Leila and Haris, and school, and everything in America. I saw the houses that my great-grandfather built when he came to Mostar from Turkey. We were lucky because none of them were bombed. At the end of the street we went to a store with ice cream and cakes where my mom used to go. It was fun getting to see her house and the things she did when she was little.

After the best ice cream in the world, we all helped clean my Grandma Zehra's house where she used to live. She had to leave it when she came to America, and it was a mess after eleven years. Grandma Zehra was back in Iowa when we were in Mostar, but Grandma Salhia, my dad's mom, was there to help us. I dusted and vacuumed, and the painters made the house look new again. Now we can stay there whenever we visit Mostar. I wish we could go back every summer. While we were cleaning, Grandma Salhia gave me some marka (📷) to get apple juice and snacks for everyone. Marka is Bosnian money—like large dollars that are green, red, or blue. After all that cleaning the house looked completely different.

The rest of the day Adi and I played soccer. We had practiced together a few times, but this was more than just kicking the ball around. It was Team Velez Day. Dad took us to the huge field for kids' try-outs. Velez is a professional soccer team for Mostar and there were signs all over that said, 'Go Velez!' The coach made us do lots of drills.

Football or Soccer?

The sport that we know as soccer in the United States is commonly called football across Europe and other parts of the world. Players try out for youth leagues in hopes of one day playing in the FIFA (Federation Internationale Football Association) World Cup Championships.

Bosnian kids playing football

'Get in front! Kick! Faster! Line up! Dribble and shoot!' he yelled in Bosnian. I was nervous, but once I got used to it, it was just like soccer in Iowa. I got to play center field. Adi was goalie. All the guys were talking football in Bosnian, and then they picked me to be captain! I played with them for a couple weeks, and they made me feel like I had always been on the team.

I'll never forget our first game against Sarajevo. We wore the real Velez team jerseys in red and white. The ref threw the ball up and we got the first kick. Someone scissor-kicked it right at me. I headed it into the net and everyone cheered. We were up 1 - 0 in the first minute! I was amazed that it went in. The game flew by. Sarajevo made lots of good shots, but Adi kept blocking them. They scored in the third period. We won, 3-2. I was so happy lining up at the end. We shook everyone's hand and said, "Dobro igra," which means 'good game.'

Afterward we celebrated with all of our relatives. My father was so proud seeing me play on the field where he learned. Just being on that field would have been great, but playing for Team Velez was the best—to fulfill my dream of playing soccer for Mostar.

It was fun to come back and tell my friends about the bridge, and soccer, and everything I did. (📷) Now when I see the picture of the Old Bridge, I know I've been there. I understand more of what my family went through. When we call our cousins, I know the things they're talking about and the kids on Adi's team. I'm proud I was there and that I got to see my relatives and the country my family is from.

Summers in Sagar

FROM INDIA TO IOWA

DES MOINES, IA

SAGAR, INDIA

FACTS ABOUT INDIA

What is the capital city?	New Delhi, population: 302,000
How far is it from Iowa?	8,635 miles
What is a favorite dessert?	Gulab juman (waffle balls)
How many people are in the country?	1.17 billion
What are common names?	Ramkumar (boys); Lakshmi (girls)

Shriya and her little sister, Anika,

kneel on the front steps of their grandparents' home in southern India. They are drawing flowers across the entryway with their mother, Savitha. The three of them dip into small pots filled with colored powder, pinching it between their fingers. First they draw a series of white dots on the ground. Then they connect them with fines lines and curves in an art form known as rangoli, [ran-GO-lee]. Shriya and Anika sprinkle each flower with blue, orange, and green powder to finish their design. Neighbors prepare their own rangoli, which adorns most every entrance along the streets of Sagar [sah-GER]. Rangoli is more than pretty artwork. It welcomes the gods in a Hindu tradition passed down through centuries. Today, visitors to Ajji and Ajja's, (grandma and grandpa's), house will admire the colorful flowers and step carefully over them as they enter. Tomorrow, Shriya and Anika will start again with a new design—and a fresh invitation to the gods.

I love India. I was born there, and every other summer we live with our grandparents in Sagar, in the state of Karnataka. When I am older I'm going to move back. I'm very close to my grandparents. Their houses are just down the street from each other. Anika and I walk between them every day and sleep at either one. At Appaji's house (which is what we call my dad's father) our uncle runs a stationery store in the front and we live in the back. (📷)

If you're walking in Sagar, there are no sidewalks and the streets are really busy. You see lots of rickshaws, and motorbikes are beeping at everyone to get out of the way. (📷) Houses and shops are all crowded together. Monkeys chatter at us and pick bananas in the trees. On our way to Appaji's house, cows walk along slowing everything down. Most people don't drive cars because streets are so narrow, and petrol (gas) is expensive. In June it's hot and monsoon season starts. It rains almost every day, more than I see in Iowa. Some days it pours heavily and some days it drizzles. Appaji says that every rain has a name that has to do with the stars. Each rain lasts three or four days and then the next one begins.

Republic of India

India is located in southern Asia. It covers 1.3 million square miles—about one-third the size of the U.S., but with four times as many people. India's population of 1.17 billion is second only to China. Approximately 70% live in rural areas, with 30% in large cities, such as India's capital of New Delhi. More than 80% of Indian people practice the religion of Hinduism. India's official language is Hindi, but all 28 states and 7 territories have their own unique languages, cultures, and cuisines. In Karnataka State, where Shriya's family is from, they speak Kannada.

India has a vast range of climates from mountains to sea level, but most of the country experiences three major seasons: a cool season from October-February; hot from March-June; and rainy monsoon season from June-September.

Hinduism

Hinduism is one of the world's oldest religions, at least 5,000 years old.

Hindus believe in a universal spirit called Brahman, sometimes referred to as God. Most believe that this spirit takes on many different forms. Hindus also believe in reincarnation, which means that when we die, we are reborn as another person, animal, or plant.

In Hinduism, there are four main deities: Brahma the creator; Vishnu the protector; Shiva the destroyer; and Shiva's wife, Shakti, (who is also called Durga or Parvati). Hindus worship at temples and usually have small shrines at home for their family deities, which they choose to worship.

In the morning, before everything gets going, we all have family jobs. The first thing is taking quick showers. We have to be clean to paint rangoli for the gods. Plus, the water only runs from 6 to 8 AM. If I don't get my shower, I have to wait 'til evening water turns on. In summertime water rations are short, so we're careful with how much we use. At Ajja and Ajji's house, my mom and uncle fill copper water pots for cooking. Then my uncle brings in armloads of firewood to heat them. If Anika and I get up early enough, we help Mom do rangoli.

My family is Hindu, and welcoming the gods is important to us. We see God in everything: sun, air, light, books, people... There are thousands of deities. Every morning and evening, whether we are in India or Iowa, we do a puja [POO-juh] at our kitchen altar. (📷) We pray to the gods that are most special to us. Since there are so many, we choose certain ones. It's our choice and our belief. I picked Ganesh, the Elephant God.

When I was little I had nightmares. To make me feel better, Mom gave me this Ganesh pendant (Shriya holds up a gold necklace with an elephant charm). It made the nightmares go away. I always wear it. I pray to him to feel safe or to do well on a test. Ganesh removes obstacles and brings protection. In India we go to his temple on Tuesdays and to temples of other gods on different days. Before entering Ganesh's temple I wash my hands and feet and take off shoes and socks. The sound of hymns playing and the smell of incense are relaxing to me. When the music ends, pujas begin. We bring fresh fruit, flowers, and sometimes peanuts for the priests to offer Ganesh. Sitting on the floor in front of his shrine, we follow along as the priests chant mantras. At the end of the service we each smear a red kumkum dot (also called a tilak) on our foreheads as a symbol of God's blessings.

Here in Iowa, instead of going to many temples, we have one Hindu temple nearby with shrines to each of the major gods. We sit on the floor with all their statues around us, called Murties. Experts came from India and spent months carving them out of black granite and white marble. I look up at the statue of Ganesh and the others with their jewels and garlands. I chant the mantras, fold my hands, and pray.

In Sagar, besides going to temples, we do pretty normal stuff—like helping with my uncle's shop and hanging out with our friends and cousins. We play hopscotch games and badminton. Anika and our little cousins play dress-up in our mom's and aunties' fancy saris, [sa-reez]. Most women like to wear saris every day. My friends and I prefer shorts and t-shirts, unless we're going to a temple or special event—like my uncle's wedding. I call him "Chikkappa," which means "little father," because he's my dad's younger brother. [chee-KA-pah] For his wedding we wore formal embroidered dresses called salwar-kameez, with long, flowing pants.

Tilak or Bindi?

In India, girls and women wear bindies on their foreheads as both a religious and fashion accent. Bindies come in many colors and stick onto the skin. A tilak is made with special red powder (kumkum) and is applied to ladies', men's, and children's foreheads at religious ceremonies, called pujas.

Anika sometimes wears a bindi on her forehead.

The Caste System

Before Chikkappa's wedding, we handed out hundreds of invitation cards around Sagar. As our tradition, we invited each family with a few grains of Akshata (rice mixed with red kumkum powder). This is to bring good luck and prosperity. My other uncle also invited all of his customers from the store. In India, each wedding is different depending on family traditions. My family arranged Chikkappa's marriage to his bride, Yamuna, [yah-MU-nah]. The first thing they did was to match his and Yamuna's horoscopes and caste [cast]. Your caste is what type of family you come from. Horoscopes predict what your life will be like based on your exact birth place, time, and date. They also tell what kind of person you should marry. Since my uncle and Yamuna were a good match, they started by seeing pictures of each other. Then our families met. After this, Yamuna and my uncle had a small engagement. In towns and villages, like Sagar, marriages are still arranged, but in large cities this is not always done. One of my aunties said that she will find a boy for me in India.

There are lots of traditions before the wedding. My personal favorite is the Henna, or mehandi, [mae-HEN-dee], as it is known in India. I couldn't wait to get it done. The only painful part was sitting still for hours while my friend, Megha, applied it. She mixed henna paste and put it in a small plastic cone. Then she drew detailed patterns on my hands, forearms, and feet. We started about 9 o'clock at night and ended at 12:30 in the morning. I had to be careful not to smear it on my bed, so I slept on my back with my arms spread out. The next morning I dusted off the dried powder. At first it looked very light. I dabbed a mixture of lemon juice and sugar over it and then rinsed it off. They say this darkens the henna and makes it last longer. It took a day or two for it to turn really dark orange. Then after a few weeks it faded.

My other favorite tradition is the bangle ceremony. All of the girls and women wear them for good luck. I love them because they jingle and they're really cool to wear. The morning before the wedding, the bangle vendor came to Appaji's house with glass bracelets in every color. (📷) I chose blue and green to match my dress. Anika and my little cousins chose green and red since that's the most popular color combination. Once I put the bangles on I had to wear them until the wedding was over. Taking them off early is bad luck. Either they have to break on their own, or you take them off at the end. To my surprise, none of them broke, and I still have them.

The day before the wedding, we rented a bus and went to Yamuna's home town for an engagement ceremony followed by a puja. Afterwards Yamuna's family put on a feast. In India, instead of getting out our best dinner plates, we eat on banana leaves for special occasions. We sat at a table lined with rows of leaves, which are even bigger than placemats. We ate many different foods—rice, curry, fruits, vegetables, sweets—all vegetarian. We always start with a bite of dessert for sweetness.

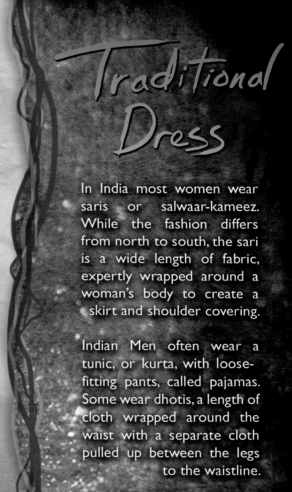

Traditional Dress

In India most women wear saris or salwaar-kameez. While the fashion differs from north to south, the sari is a wide length of fabric, expertly wrapped around a woman's body to create a skirt and shoulder covering.

Indian Men often wear a tunic, or kurta, with loose-fitting pants, called pajamas. Some wear dhotis, a length of cloth wrapped around the waist with a separate cloth pulled up between the legs to the waistline.

Then we eat the main courses before finishing dessert. The next day, Chikkappa and Yamuna were married in a big celebration with over a thousand guests. Two days later, my dad's family hosted a reception to welcome them into Appaji's home. Along with a special rangoli across the entry (), we decorated the doorway with mango leaves and flowers. We put the red kumkum on their foreheads, and Yamuna "Chikki" (which means auntie) officially joined our family with another party that lasted into the night.

My wedding could be like this: my relatives will help my parents find a guy in India that suits me. Then I'll get to decide whether I like him or not. When I tell my Iowa friends this, even my girlfriends from India, they say: 'You have to pick your own husband.' They say that arranged marriages are not the way it is done now. But it's our tradition.

In Shriya's future, she sees the possibility of becoming a doctor or an engineer. She talks about moving back to India, and an arranged marriage, as if she can see what lies ahead. At the same time she knows that her pathway could lead to many places, just as her father's career led her family to Iowa. For Shriya, one thing is certain: she treasures her friends, family, and summers in Sagar.

Where the Flowers Are

AN AMERICAN TELLING OF A SUDANESE TALE

DES MOINES, IA

MAYENTHON, SUDAN

FACTS ABOUT SUDAN

What is the capital city?	Khartoum, population: 639,598
How far is it from Iowa?	7,220 miles
What is a favorite afternoon snack?	*Sohleb*, sorghum pudding with ginger
How many people are in the country?	42.3 million
What are common names?	Ayen (girls), Mayon (boys)

Under the acacia trees

by the river, the cattle tuck their hooves beneath them after their evening milking, shutting their eyes in the cool of the day. (📷) Nearby, children splash and giggle at the shallow riverbank while mothers pour water over the cooking fires. A new moon and a few early stars have gathered in the indigo sky over the village of Mayenthon, home to the Dinka [DEENG-ka] tribe of southern Sudan. Dau is the first one at the gathering place in his father's courtyard. It is his favorite time of day.

I was front and center at evening storytelling. My father and grandfather, Beruba the storyteller, and the other men gathered, speaking in low voices about important matters of the day. When they saw me waiting, they smiled and shook their heads. I just shrugged and

smiled back at them. I had fed the chickens and watered the garden. I had finished all of my sums for Sister Jacqueline. I had even scrubbed Kacuol [kok WOL] and Jok-Jok behind the ears as mother had asked.

Finally, my mother and aunties and the younger children returned from the river. They carried clean pots, food pouches, water gourds, and the babies strapped to their backs. When I saw them I got up and marked my place on the ground with a big letter D. (📷) Then I ran to help my mother with Alek, my baby sister.

Soon my father and grandfather lit the torches all around the compound. The other kids scrambled to find a place up front while the mothers and babies got settled in the back. Beruba is the oldest man in our village, so he has the most stories to tell. Suddenly, baby Alek fussed out loud. Mother

looked sharp at me. Alek had a tooth coming in, so I crooked my thumb for her to soothe her gums on the knucklebone. That way I wouldn't have to miss a word of Beruba's story:

Once upon a time there was a boy who lived a perfect life in the village where he was born. His father was a wealthy man with many head of cattle and many faithful servants. His mother tended beautiful gardens and was known all around for her delicious cooking. In the dry season, the

villagers camped on the banks of a fat river where they drank and washed and played and watered the cattle. In the rainy season, their tightly woven huts kept them warm and dry. There were many children and many elders and everyone always had enough to eat.

One day, bad men came to the village--raiders who steal and kill. The boy hid in a large grain basket in his father's house, shuddering from fear. When he finally dared to leave his hiding place, the village elders came to him. "Your mother and father and brothers and sisters are all gone. Everything is destroyed. You must leave here at once," they told him. "You must find a way to imagine a new village to replace the old one."

"Imagine a new village?" asked the grieving boy.

"The spirits of the grassland and the cattle are magical," they told him. "You can imagine a different story with new grasslands, new cattle to graze in the camps by the river, and new woven huts to protect us during the rainy season."

"But how can I replace all of the things our people have lost?"

The elders replied, "Your thoughts will make it so. You must go where there are feelings and color. Go where there are flowers. And then you will return to us and all of this will be new."

It was the strangest story Beruba had ever told. I couldn't stop thinking about this boy. We Dinka are warriors, but the elders expected that boy to save his village by leaving it. He had to use his imagination, not guns. But I knew the storytellers were smart. They don't have books; they just know the stories. Sometimes

Storytelling is a living tradition for most Africans. Everyone participates in the interactive performance of a story, which often includes song and dance. The celebrated African novelist, Chinua Achebe wrote "It is the story that outlives the sound of war-drums and the exploits of brave fighters….The story is our escort; without it, we are blind."

Children play in the river before storytelling begins.

we had festivals, and there would be stories day and night, like twelve in a row. Some were fiction—stories about magical lions or cattle that could talk. But some were true.

When I was small, the storytellers told tales of the long-ago Dinka as God's favored people—we call ourselves Mounyjaang [moon-ya-JONG]. Then came troubled times. Many people came to my father seeking work or food. Some days we weren't allowed to leave the compound because of rumors that raiders were coming to kill and destroy everything. As our lives changed, the stories changed, too. The endings weren't always happy. Then came the night Beruba told the story about the boy whose village was destroyed. That was the first time I really thought that we might have to go away. I think African people have the sense that when they create stories, they make the truth. Things did happen in Mayenthon like in the story that Beruba told, and we did have to leave because of the war. We are a scattered people.

Now I am in the eighth grade at Holy Family School in Des Moines, Iowa. My language arts teacher gave me a book, *The Giver*, by Lois Lowery. I was so surprised because the story was familiar, like the story Beruba told. It is about a boy who lives in a place where life seems perfect. But then he finds out that his world is built on lies, all lies. He is called to become the Receiver of Memory for his people, but he is forced to leave home. At first the boy is lost and very sad. He must live with danger, hunger and uncertainty. Then he discovers color and feelings, animals and seasons. This boy believes he can make a better life. In Beruba's story, too, the boy finds the place where the flowers are, the place he had been told to imagine, where he could live free.

Dau lives with his family in a big old house just a few blocks from the local university. His mother has a small garden in the backyard, and the living room is trimmed with brightly colored plastic flowers that help to welcome friends. Since Martin Luther King Jr. Boulevard is a busy street, Dau falls asleep to the sounds of traffic.

Some nights I wake up and it takes me a while to remember I am not in Mayenthon. I don't hear the quiet sky or the hyenas crying in the distance. I hear horns honking, television, or fire sirens. I sit up in bed and check on Jok Jok and Alek. Back home, I had to hide them more than once, in a grain basket or the cistern, when bad men came to our village. I told them they had to not make a sound.

I was born in Khartoum [kar-TOOM], the capitol of Sudan, but because of the war, my father, a military officer, wanted to raise us in the countryside. He grew rice, corn, wheat, tomatoes, peanuts, and anyanjang [on-yon-JONG], which is called millet in English, as well as 200 head of cows and

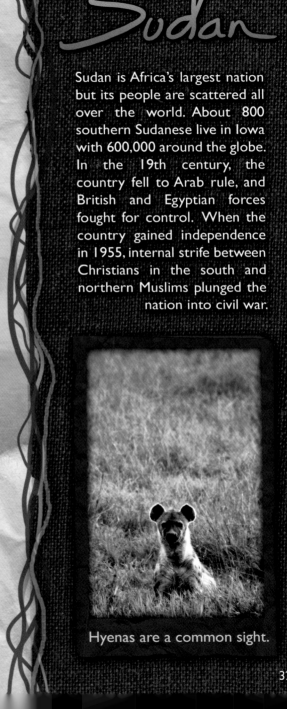

Sudan

Sudan is Africa's largest nation but its people are scattered all over the world. About 800 southern Sudanese live in Iowa with 600,000 around the globe. In the 19th century, the country fell to Arab rule, and British and Egyptian forces fought for control. When the country gained independence in 1955, internal strife between Christians in the south and northern Muslims plunged the nation into civil war.

Hyenas are a common sight.

many goats. Our huts are made of a sturdy, tightly woven grass. When the rainy season is about to come we plant this grass, which grows wild like the rain. If it's not a lucky year then you can't do anything about it. The crops will die. Our livestock live in a separate hut plastered with thick mud to keep the cattle in—and the tigers out! In my tribe, cattle are not just animals; they are our wealth. (📷) Nowadays, there is hardly any cattle left.

In the summer, nobody wants to sleep inside, so we hang mosquito nets from stakes built into the walls of the compound. Nearby the compound are two watering holes, one for people and one for the animals. () When it gets really dry, sometimes you have to share the watering hole with the animals. It is not as safe to drink, but when you are thirsty you don't have any choice.

Years ago,

Dau's father had thought about leaving Africa and bringing the family to the United States. But he believed he should stay in Sudan to fight for his people. In the end, the family did come to the US. But Dau never dreamed it would take his father's death to make it happen.

I was six years old. I was helping Dad and Grandpa plant peanuts in the dirt and laughing at Dubu, my dad's spoiled pet goat. Dad's bodyguards had Dubu on a rope, but the goat tugged hard and wriggled his lips trying to get the peanuts out of my planting bag, hollering "MEEE! MEEE!" We were having fun teasing Dubu when my auntie came out to the garden, weeping. She told my father her husband was in trouble. Grandpa told my dad not to trust auntie's husband because he was a bad man. But Dad went and changed into his military uniform and left with his bodyguards. I stood there holding Dubu's rope. It was the last time I saw my father. At the watering hole where he went to help auntie's husband, a bad man who worked for the enemy shot him from a hiding spot. Auntie's

husband had tricked him. On the day of the funeral, Grandpa killed the fat and spoiled Dubu. (📷) "Don't cry," Grandpa told me. "Now your father will have a buddy in heaven."

We had to stop going to school. My dad's bodyguards went away and everyone who had worked for him went to my uncle. Grandpa did everything he could to help, but eventually my mother decided she must find a better life for us.

When I was nine years old, Mother took us—me, Kacuol, Jok-Jok, and baby Alek to a refugee camp in Uganda. (📷) There we attended Catholic school. We spoke Dinka at home and had to learn Swahili [swa-HEEL-li] for school.

It was about two years of waiting. It's hard to get into the United States. Finally, on the 5th of December we flew from Kampala, Uganda to London, to New York City, to Chicago, and finally to Des Moines. I was eleven years old. When we got to Iowa I was so surprised. I thought America was full of skyscrapers and busy streets and crowds, like New York City. But I saw big sky, fields, tall trees and a big fat river—just like home.

In just two years

Dau learned to speak fluently, just as he had learned to speak Swahili in Uganda. At school, his favorite subject is religion, and he is just one player away from the top spot on the school's basketball team. Even though Dau is glad to be in Iowa, Dau's thoughts often turn towards his native Sudan.

I think about all of the people I used to live with like my grandma and grandpa. The old people lost most of their children in the war. They need little things like sugar and cheese, clothes and shoes and pencils—lots of things that we just throw away. I believe that my father would have wanted me to go back to help my people. Almost every day I think about Beruba's story of the boy who was the Receiver of Memory for his people and had to imagine a new village to replace the old one. I wonder if I am like that boy.

A lot of my friends from other tribes forget about where they come from. They make trouble at home. They talk bad to each other and even to the teachers. Some boys my age "forget" how to say almost everything but "kudual" [koo-DWAL] (hello) or "loi adi?" [lo-ee ODD-ee] (how are you). I speak the Dinka language, we call it thuong jang [thoo-ong-JONG] most of the time except for at school.

Dowry Dance

The Dinka tradition of the dowry dance is good jumping practice. During a Dinka dowry dance, men try to jump the highest to impress the women and family of the potential brides-to-be. So the men of Dau's tribe—already tall people—would have lots of practice in jumping high, and that would come in handy on any basketball team.

A Dinka jumping contest.

When I talk with people who knew my father they have high expectations for me to finish my studies. I think my dad would want me to finish college. But I also think he would want me to make my own decisions. Even when I was little I used to get these big pictures in my head. I would think about earning big money to go and buy a bus in Africa and help all the people who are being displaced from their countries. I wish I could be like Beruba; I wish I could tell a story that would make it so.

I started playing basketball at school. Some kids told me I stank at it and I wanted to get better. I started to go to the YMCA everyday. Some of the other kids watched me play and said, "You need to pass like this," or "You need to move the ball faster." I started to take their advice. I had so much to learn. Now I play for Holy Family. Next year when I go to high school, I hope to play for Roosevelt.

My uncle is Manute Bol, the famous center for the Washington Bullets. (📷) He was the first foreign draft in the NBA. He's retired now, but he still holds the league record for blocking the most shots per minute. My dream is to play professional basketball like my uncle. If my work pays off maybe I can go to the pros like he did. I would do like my uncle did and help the poor people of my country.

My life would be very different if I had stayed in Mayenthon. I would have the choice to become a parapuol [PARE-a-pwol], a boy warrior-protector of my tribe and our cattle. You have to be very tough to go through the challenge. You fight a lot of boxing matches with other boys to see who is the leader. In the end, there is a ceremony. They make the cuts on the forehead (📷) and you don't want to flinch or cry because then everyone will remember that about you for the rest of your life. When I was in Africa, I was too young to try to become a parapuol. Now I don't have the choice. But I still want to help to protect my people.

Division in Sudan

Sudan is an Arab country under Muslim rule. The Sudan People's Liberation Movement/Army is made up of people from the south of Sudan, who are mostly Christian. Together with the National Democratic Alliance group, the SPLM/A signed a peace agreement that will allow the newly formed Government of Southern Sudan (GOSS) to seek its independence from Sudan beginning in 2011.

The first step is to get an education. One of Dau's heroes, an inspirational leader of his people named John Garang who died in 2005, was a Dinka who attended Grinnell College in Iowa. Perhaps Dau will go to college here in Iowa, as well.

Emelia, Dau's mother, is preparing for a trip back to Sudan soon. She has been appointed to a parliamentary seat by the new leader of the Sudanese People's Liberation Movement. Recently, she achieved her United States citizenship. Now she is able to travel back and forth between the U.S. and Sudan in her role as a representative for the concerns of Sudanese women and children.

My mom was asked to serve because my dad fought so hard for our people. I think that's cool. I cannot go back yet because I have to go to school. I wish I could see my grandparents and Beruba and just remember what it is like to be African in Africa.

When you're just a little kid you think the place where you were born is the place where your memories will always be. I thought I would be in that village forever. Now only God knows what is coming for me.

For Dau, Iowa is where the flowers are, a place where there is hope for a better life. His mother's parliamentary work is an example of that hope for the future, just as his father's work was to bring hope to his people. Dau is growing up in America, but he will always be a part of the village, the stories, and the country he left behind. (📷)

Little Dutch Girl

FROM THE NETHERLANDS TO IOWA

THE NETHERLANDS

DES MOINES, IA

FACTS ABOUT THE NETHERLANDS

What is the capital city?	Amsterdam, 762,000
How far is it from Iowa?	4,371 miles
What is a favorite afternoon snack?	Salmiakki (salty liquorice)
How many people in the country?	16.6 million
What are the most common names?	Daan and Sem (boys); Sophie and Julia (girls)

If you were standing

at the Snow Rock Dairy farm after a big rain, you could look down and see a bright sky and puffy clouds reflected in the puddles all around you. But if a calf moos and the farm cats scatter, watch out! Here comes Jenny Reuling wearing tall rubber boots and a great big grin, and she's about to splash droplets of clouds and sky everywhere. When the puddles are still again, a big wide barn, a yellow house with a wrap-around porch, and a flourishing kitchen garden come into view. Jenny's dad chugs up on his tractor, where he's looking out over the field of tall corn that borders his farm. Snow Rock Dairy is home to 300 milking cows and the Reuling family: Jenny, her Dad, Eduard, her mom, Resy, and her little sister and brothers. Nine-year-old Jenny looks like any Iowa farm girl, only she's not from Iowa.

When my mom and dad first told me we were leaving home to go to America, I didn't want to come. I was only five years old, and I didn't want to say goodbye to my grandma and grandpa and my cousin, Inge. She's the same age as me, and she's my best friend. But then Mom told me I would get to ride on a big airplane. I liked that idea. I have never been to school in the Netherlands because we moved to Iowa right before I was supposed to start kindergarten. On the first

day I felt shy and I didn't want to learn English. I just copied what everyone else did. I didn't understand anything. A teacher came two times a week to help me with flash cards. She always brought me a stuffed bunny to play with. I learned English pretty fast and even helped my mom with translating papers that my teacher sent home. Now I'm in the fifth grade at Washington Irving Elementary School in Waverly. I'm just like the American kids and I don't remember very much about when I lived in the Netherlands. But I still think of myself as Dutch.

It was different for my little sister Ryanna, who was only three when we moved here. She learned to speak Dutch and English at the same time. Nicklaus and Wouter, my baby brothers, were born in Iowa. Nicklaus doesn't remember the Netherlands at all because we only visited once before he could walk. Wouter has never even been to the Netherlands. Of course, my brothers speak mostly English, but we speak Dutch to them because we want them to know they are Dutch--Dutch and American.

The Reulings came to Iowa as part of the Iowa New Farm Family Project, a program in which dairy farmers from the Netherlands are invited by an Iowa "host county" to build their dairy business in a community that will benefit from their industry. Back in the Netherlands, available land to pasture cows is very limited. Dairy farming families cannot thrive or pass their businesses to the next generation. Iowa has everything they need: plenty of land, water, feed, and a market for milk products. The Reulings were the first family to participate in the program.

I've never milked a cow the old-fashioned way. My dad had to do that when he was growing up. We use machines because we have a lot of cows. They stand in a pen and you attach a pump to their teats. It doesn't hurt them. You have to get up really early, like 4 or 5 o-clock in the morning, and

Most of the Netherlands is well below sea level ("nether" means low) and it has actually been sinking slowly for centuries. Now, climate change is making the seas rise even faster. Fierce storms pound the southwest coastline for much of the year as the land mass gradually diminishes. In response, the Dutch have engineered the world's biggest seawall along their coastline, called the Deltawerken. They have even begun to build whole towns on stilts and towns that float. But because land is growing limited and the country has a dense population, dairy farming is also limited. That's one reason why the Reuling family came to farm in Iowa.

The New Family Farm

When Jenny grows up she and all her siblings will have the right to remain in the U.S. if they choose. The New Family Farm Project is a conditional immigration program that makes it possible for farmers to invest in Iowa what they would have invested back home. According to Paul Brown of the Iowa State Extension, Iowa needs their investment and knowledge because we have skipped a generation of farmers. The families are only allowed to resettle in 77 approved counties that have undergone extensive planning and preparation. In order to achieve permanent residence, the families must pay taxes, create a minimum of ten jobs for the local economy and invest at least $500,000 in their Iowa farm.

then you have to milk them again in the evening. Did you know cows can stand up just hours after they are born? It seems like they are always born in the middle of the night. When that happens my mom goes out and sits with them. My dad lets us have a cow for a pet. My favorite was named Labby, one of the first ones on the farm. I loved her because she was different from the other cows. She was a Holstein-

Jersey crossbreed, very sweet, with big eyes. But she got sick and the vet couldn't make her better, so we had to say goodbye.

Some people might think there's nothing to do on a farm, but I like living in the country. We help my mom grow squashes and pumpkins and sunflowers and cucumbers and tomatoes. The rabbits get a lot of it, but that's all right. We have a giant jungle-gym and we can swing high and scream our heads off because there's just big quiet all around. My dad takes us for rides on the tractor. We play tag and verstoppertje [ver-STOP-er-juh] – what American kids call hide-and-seek.

It took me a while to understand some of the American holidays, like Halloween: so you get to make up a costume like a witch or a maybe a princess. It can be scary but it doesn't have to be. Then you have to bring some treats to your class and bring a bucket for more treats, and then you come home with your bucket filled with treats from the other

kids. It doesn't have to be a bucket; it could be a bag or a plastic pumpkin instead. I don't get the point of Halloween but it's fun to dress up and get candy. We don't really have Thanksgiving in the Netherlands, or Valentine's Day. Christmas is a little bit different in the Netherlands. We have Sinterklass instead of Santa Claus. He's more like Saint Nicholas.

And of course we have birthday parties. This is how we sing "Happy Birthday":

Lang zal ze leven (Let her live long)
Lang zal ze leven (Let her live long)
Lang zal ze leven in de Gloria (Let her live long in glory)
In de glo-ri-a, in de
glo-ri-a (In gloy, in glory)
Hiep-hiep-hiep hoera! (Hip-hip hooray!)
Hiep-hiep-hiep hoera! (Hip-hip hooray!)

It's different for girls than it is for boys: you say *hij leven* [hidge LAYven] instead of *ze leven* [zuh LAYven] for them. My teacher always asks me to sing the birthday song to my class. We sing it in different languages depending on where everyone is from, so that means Chinese, Spanish, Dutch and English. At school, the other kids are always asking me how to say words

Here Comes Sinterklaas

This Dutch figure, named after Saint Nicholas, the patron saint of children and sailors, is the origin of the American Santa Claus. In the Netherlands, Saint Nicholas Day is celebrated on the eve of December 5 and December 6. Like Santa Claus, Sinterklass brings presents through the chimney. He rides on a gray steed, not a reindeer and his "elf" does the work. And he didn't come from the North Pole, by sleigh, but from Spain, by steamboat.

Holland and the Netherlands

Many people think Holland is the old-fashioned word for the Netherlands, but Holland is actually the central-western part of the Netherlands. The Netherlands (Nederland, in Dutch) is the European portion of the Kingdom of the Netherlands that is formed by the Netherlands and two Caribbean islands, the Netherlands Antilles and Aruba. The Netherlands seat of government is called The Hague, but the capital is Amsterdam. The Hague is also home to the International Court of Justice of the United Nations.

Dutch shoes called clogs.

in Dutch, like "girl" which is meisje [MAYja] or "boy" which is jongen [YOUNGun]. The funny thing is some of the words are really almost the same, like vriend is "friend" (it's vriendin if it's a girl, though) and koe is "cow." I like speaking more than one language and being able to translate. When I get to be "star of the week" at school, I like to show pictures of my cousins and the place where I was born. And I send pictures to Inge, too. She likes the one where I am racing Ryanne across the barn on our Big Wheels. I even had time to stop and pick up the tiger-striped farm cat, and I still won. When we aren't racing we sometimes like to get in the calf pen. The calves are in there together because they have to be weaned from their mothers a few weeks after they are born. The computer chips on their ears keep track of how much the calves are eating and how fast they are gaining weight. The program builds the amount of milk up and weans them also. Calves grow pretty fast. (📷) Their coats look really soft but they have to get tough because they are out here all winter. It gets cold and pretty muddy when it's not icy.

When I grow up I think I would like to live on a farm, not in the city where it's crowded. I like school a lot, so I would like to be a teacher. I really like to read—I could read for hours and hours if my brothers and sister would let me. And I'm learning to play the flute. My cousin,

Inge, once played for us on Skype—that's how we keep in touch with everyone back home—and when I saw her playing I wanted to learn, too. I really like being back in the Netherlands. Next year we are going to go back to visit again, and I will get to be with Inge and my other cousins, Jelmar and Mathijs. It's nice that we are friends with the other Dutch families here that also came as part of the Farm Family program. Some of them are having a hard time because the milk prices aren't good right now.

Over one hundred and fifty years ago, the Dutch were some of the first settlers in central Iowa and started some of the very same towns and farms where the new farm families have now settled. And there was probably a Dutch girl from the Netherlands who came to Iowa with her family and wasn't so sure she was ready to say goodbye to the only life she had ever known. She probably wasn't wearing blue jeans and a tee shirt or riding a Big Wheel through puddles in the open barn. But she probably helped in the kitchen garden and chased the farm cats and maybe even milked the cows the old-fashioned way. Today, Jenny isn't really thinking about the 1860s. She is thinking about this weekend, and her first sleepover with her friend, Cloey, from school. It's Cloey's

Dutch Doughnuts Recipe

- 1 (0.6 ounce) cake compressed fresh yeast
- 1 cup lukewarm milk/water
- 2 1/4 cups all-purpose flour
- 2 teaspoons salt
- 1 egg
- 3/4 cup dried currants
- 3/4 cup raisins
- 1 teaspoon orange rind
- 1 Granny Smith apple (peeled, cored, finely chopped)
- 1 quart vegetable oil for deep-frying
- 1 cup confectioners' sugar for dusting

Mix flour, yeast, salt, raisins, apple, orange rind, and liquid. Cover the bowl and let the yeast rise at least 30 minutes in a warm pot. Scoop the batter with an ice-cream scoop and cook in hot vegetable oil in a deep-fryer for 5-8 minutes. Let them cool on paper towels, then dust with powdered sugar. Best served hot. (📷)

English Only

In the mid-1800s, the state's Board of Immigration published booklets in German, Dutch, Danish, and Swedish encouraging immigration to Iowa. By the late 1800's, Europeans were immigrating in large numbers. Most could not speak English. Just like many immigrants of today, the parents had to work so hard to make a living that there was little time for learning a new language. Their children, who learned English in school, translated for their parents. But some native-born Iowans felt hostility toward these new citizens with their foreign language and customs. In 1918, an "English only" law banned any language other than English for a time.

birthday, and she's looking forward to hearing the birthday song in Dutch.

I read a story at the library about a boy who stuck his finger in a hole in the sea wall to keep the water from leaking in. (📷) The story was called The Little Dutch Boy. Most Dutch people don't even know that story. It's just one of the things Americans think of when they think about Dutch people. There's a town in Iowa called Pella that's full of Dutch-type things because it was started by Dutch people in Iowa a long time ago. We haven't been there yet, but we want to see it. I heard that they have really good bakeries in Pella. I hope they have oliebollen. These are sweet dumplings with bits of fruit in them that you fry in hot oil. What you call doughnuts, I think. My mom makes them every December 31st to celebrate the New Year. I remember more about the Netherlands than Ryanne, Nicklaus, and Wouter because I'm the oldest. I'm glad I speak Dutch and remember where I'm from. I don't want to lose it.

Dremali Street

FROM GAZA TO DES MOINES, IOWA

DES MOINES, IA

GAZA

FACTS ABOUT PALESTINE

When did the country gain independence?	Gaza City, population: 449,221
How far is it from Iowa?	6,427 miles
What is a favorite afternoon snack?	*Timriyyeh*, a pudding pastry fried in sesame oil
How many people in the country?	4,043,218 (Palestine Territories)
What are the most common names?	Ahmad (boys), Faiza (girls)

Ten-year-old Rashad Dremali

peers out from the front step of his father's childhood home on his first morning in Gaza, Palestine. The sun has not quite risen beyond the mosque on the hill, but already the sky is blue and bright. Rashad can smell the ocean in a soft breeze. (📷) He shades his eyes and squints to see a row of block style houses of white painted stone. Inside each of the homes that line this street lives someone Rashad is related to—his uncles and aunties, his first cousins and his father's cousins, his nieces and nephews. He sits down to lace up his shoes. He can't wait to meet everyone.

My father told me, "Enter any house on this street, and you will be welcomed as family." After I had been there a few days I realized he really meant it, and I started to get more comfortable. Uncle Kamil told me that if I felt like watching television in his big leather chair, I should just walk across the street, sit down, and pick up the remote. Another time, I

knocked on Auntie Fadwa's door, and she had a plate of the world's best musakhkhan, [MOO-sock-on] a spicy chicken and vegetable dish, for me when I stepped inside. My cousins were the best, though. Nazir and Bashira and I spent whole days at the beach, competing to see who could dig the deepest hole and find treasure. The sand is really golden there, not white like back home in Florida, and underneath the sand are tons of ruins of ancient Palestinian civilization. I was thousands of miles from Fort Lauderdale, Florida, where I was born, but everyone made me feel like they had known me my entire life.

The Gaza Strip

The Gaza Strip is located inside Palestine and is therefore governed by the state of Israel. But Palestinians do not recognize the authority of Israel because they believe their land was taken from them by the Israelis. This conflict has caused much bloodshed since 1948, when Israel first attempted to occupy Palestine. Except for the Gaza Strip, the occupation was complete. The battle between the Israelis and Palestinians for control over this region continues.

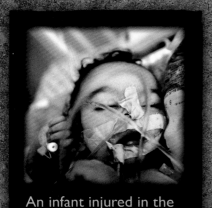

An infant injured in the violent war in Gaza

Everyone on Dremali Street made me feel at home. But I'm glad I don't live there. My father's family is there—five brothers and a sister. He sends money so that they can build a big, sturdy house because they never know when their part of the city will be bombed. Lately they have to use the money just to live. When your city is a war zone, it's hard to find everyday things. There is trouble in the world. But my father expects us to hold to what is good. That is what the Qur'an [koor-ON] teaches us.

"Here, people create their own opportunity," my father says. That's why my parents came to Florida in 1986. He was the imam, the religious leader, at the mosque in Boca Raton, Florida. But my brother got into bad fights with boys who gave him trouble. People would say stuff to my mom, even in the grocery store. It got so bad my father decided to home-school us for a while. Then in 2005, he answered a call for an imam at the Islamic Center of Des Moines. We didn't know anything about Iowa, but my father wanted his children to be safe.

I had really close friends back in Florida. And on the other side of the world on Dremali Street there was a street full of people who already loved me. I knew there was no way my new street in Des Moines would be anything like that.

In the winter of 2005,

Rashad's parents, Ibrahim [EE-bra-heem] and Saafa [SAW-fa], his elder brother, Fayed and his younger brother and sister, Omar, age 7 and Haza, age 5, moved to Des Moines, Iowa in a neighborhood not far from the Islamic Center where Ibrahim became the new imam. Iowans have been generous and open people who have reached out to the Dremalis in many ways.

The first time I met my best friend in Iowa, we were enemies. After my first day of school here, this boy I had never met came up to me and pushed me. He dared me to fight. I refused. Then a few days later after gym class, I saw this same kid getting picked on by two eighth-grade boys. "Hey, leave him alone," I told the older boys.

"What do you care?" one of them sneered at me. "I saw him knock you down the other day."

"Yeah," the other bully said. "Do you like getting pushed around?"

"No one likes getting pushed around," I answered. "That's why I'm telling you to leave him alone. This kid's my friend."

"Yeah, right," said the first kid. "You don't even know his name."

I remembered what the coach had called him: "It's Amiel," I said.

The coach came into the locker rooms after that and the eighth-graders scrambled. Amiel looked at me. "What'd you do that for?"

"When you fight back," I told him, "that's how wars get started."

Ever since that day, we've been good friends. I like to have friends from a lot of different backgrounds. I met my friend, Matthew, one day when I was shooting hoops. My friend, Harris, is in eighth grade and likes to play pool. Together, Amiel, Matthew, Harris and I are like the Four Stooges.

My friends like to hang out at the mosque [mosk]. Even if my dad's on the phone or leading

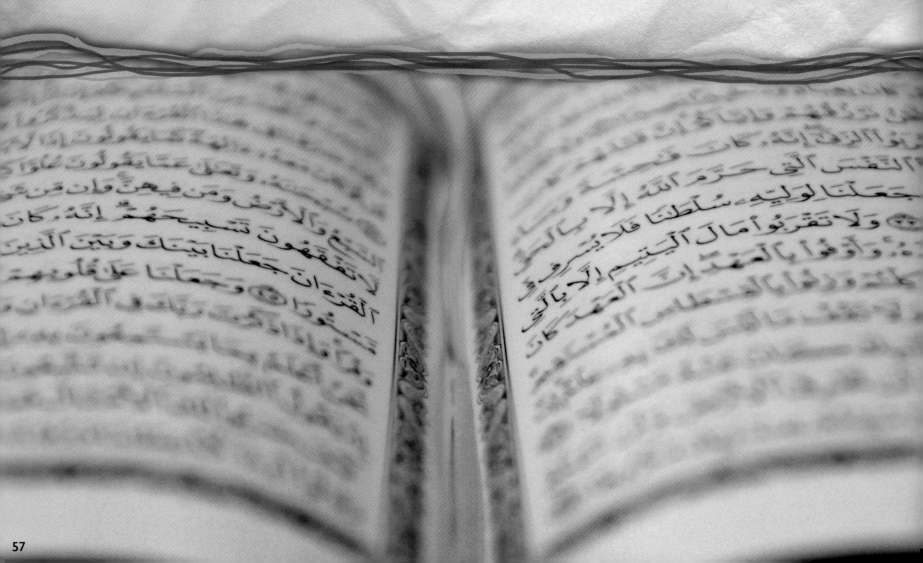

prayer service when they come, they know they are still welcome. They come to see my Jaddah [ja-DAH], grandmother, who feeds them and fusses over them. They are my friends, so in her eyes they can do no wrong. Jaddah is so happy here.

The Dremalis' home has Saafa, Rashad's mother's, touch. On the wall in the living room is a gold-leaf painting of the great work of Islamic architecture called the Dome of the Rock (📷), known in Arabic as Qubbat al-Sakhrah [KOOB-at-al-SOCK-rah]. Built in the last years of 600 A.D., this building is said to house the site from which the Prophet Mohammed ascended through the seven heavens into the presence of Allah [ah-LAH] the God of Islam. Rashad has brought this painting and other items to school to share with his teacher and classmates.

The word "Islam" comes from the Arabic word for peace. It means "to achieve peace" or "to surrender." Our holy book is called the Qur'an, which is the word of Allah that was revealed to the Prophet Mohammed. These words and teachings are called Sunnah. It is told in surahs, which are numbered passages similar to verses in the Bible. Some of the stories are the same, too, like the story of Noah and the Ark. I have to memorize the entire Qur'an in Arabic. (📷) It's not as hard as it sounds because the surahs are short. I listen to them on my iPod when I'm lying on my bed or doing laps for gym.

My mom says life is a test, and Allah allows us to make

A Muslim is a person who follows the religion of Islam, a world religion with roots in the same sources as both Judaism and Christianity. One fifth of the world is Muslim, with believers on every continent of the globe. Indonesians, not Arabs, make up the majority of believers. Muslims adhere to the Five Pillars of Islam. They must profess their faith, which is called shahada [SHA-ha-DAH]. They must pray, called salat [sahl-OT]. They must give to charity and help the poor, called zakat [zah-KAHT]. They must fast during Ramadan, called sawm. And at least once in their life, they must perform the Hajj [HOD-je] which is the pilgrimage to the holy city of Mecca [mek-KAH] located in Saudi Arabia.

The Great Mosque in Mecca

Muslim Prayer

How do Muslims pray? What do they pray about? Wherever they are in the world, Muslims always turn toward Mecca to pray. Prayer involves crossing the hands, raising the hands, chanting, kneeling and prostrating one's self (lying forward on the floor). These actions are repeated many times during prayer. The main prayer that Muslims say, often many times a day, is called the Fathia. Similar to the Lord's Prayer, which all Christians know, the Fathia is the prayer that every Muslim knows.

A muslim praying on a mat.

mistakes because he wants to see what quality of people we are. She doesn't like us to watch the news or worry about things we hear. But we do hear about some bombings and killings in the news, sometimes right in Gaza City. My dad calls home to his brothers. "Are you all right?" he asks them. "Can you go out at all?" I don't get it. How can we say that good always triumphs over evil? Both Islam and Judaism say this. Which one is right? We are all human beings. We are all created equal.

The first time I invited my friend Carter for a sleepover, his parents rushed over to the house. They didn't know anything about Muslims and looked nervous standing out there on the front porch. Then they met my mom and dad, my grandmother and Farek and Omar and Haza. They saw we were just like them, a nice family.

Being Muslim is not just about my religion, though. It is our whole life. It's how we live. I had a friend who disrespected his mom almost every day. My dad didn't want me to be friends with him anymore because in Islam, the obedience of the children to the parents is very important.

Muslims pray five times a day: before sunrise, at mid-day, in the afternoon, when the sun goes down, and before bed. To pray, you turn toward Mecca, the holy city of Islam, which is in Saudi Arabia. Before you pray, you should wash your face, hands, and head and feet. It's best to pray in the mosque, but that isn't always possible. On school days after lunch, I just pray sitting at my desk. If I were sitting next to you, you wouldn't even know I was praying. Sometimes I get involved in what I'm doing and forget what time it is. Even though my friends aren't all Muslim, they're pretty good at keeping me on track. Once, I got to a really high level on a math game and I didn't want to stop. Carter leaned over to me and asked, "Isn't it time for you to pray?" I was about to pass his highest level on the game. That's why he wanted me to stop and pray.

I shrugged him off. I was too close to stop now.

"Rashad!" Carter shouted just when I topped his last best score. He took off his shoe and threw it at me. I ducked and it hit my poster of Sami Yusuf, a Muslim pop singer I like. "Beat that score," I said smiling and handing him the game. Then I got down on my rug and bowed toward Mecca.

One of the most important times of the year for Muslims is the holy festival of Ramadan [ROM-a-don]. When Rashad's classmates ask him why he doesn't eat or drink anything at school during this month, he explains that Muslims fast from sunrise to sunset. Fasting reminds them to turn to Allah for all that they need and to appreciate their blessings.

Ramadan

Ramadan is the ninth month of the Islamic Calendar, when Muslims practice the fourth pillar of Islam, fasting, or sawm. Muslims believe that during the month of Ramadan, Allah revealed the first verses of the Qur'an, the holy book of Islam. But because the Islamic calendar is based on the moon and not the sun, it is 11 days shorter than the solar calendar. Thus, the period of Ramadan (29 or 30 days) remains the same, but the month in which it occurs during the solar calendar changes every year.

Muslims celebrating the end of Ramadan.

Fasting is about more than not eating food. You are supposed to fast from all bad habits, like lying or cheating or drinking too much soda. The whole point of Ramadan is to be reminded of those who go without. It gets really hard some days, especially at first. But you learn patience. It softens you, in a way…softens your heart. We all fast together, even my little brother and sister, Omar and Haza, a little bit. It teaches us to be grateful that we have food to turn from when others truly don't have food.

I don't make a big deal of fasting at school. I just stay in the resource room and read or get ahead on my homework. They even give me permission to get out of gym class because of not eating, but no way am I going to miss basketball or soccer practice after school.

The end of Ramadan is a fun and special day called Eid-al-Fitr [EYE-doll-fit-EAR] when you break the fast and have a big party with loads of food. (📷) On Eid-al-Fitr we get up really early because we want to eat as soon as possible! We pray and then say "Eid Mubarak" to greet each other. This just means something like "happy holiday." We attend the prayer service and repeat the Takbirat [tock-BEER-ott] which is when we chant ALLAH AKBAR, "Allah is the greatest!" Then the fun really starts. At the mosque, the basement is filled with delicious cooking smells. Everyone's mood is the best because we had our patience tested during Ramadan and now we feel free.

Like a lot of 7th graders at Urbandale Middle School, Rashad plays football, basketball, and soccer, enjoys skateboarding and practices karate. He wants to be just like his dad when he grows up. But it's not every 7th grader who gets up in front of a hundred people to share his thoughts about peace. On a blustery March morning not long ago, Rashad Dremali, age 11, spoke at a peace rally in downtown Des Moines. (*)*

My dad had been asked to speak at the anniversary of the start of the war in Iraq, and he invited me to come along. There was a march around downtown Des Moines first, and I helped carry the flag of Palestine next to some others who were carrying the American flag. My dad talked about the need to understand and respect the different world religions because we live in

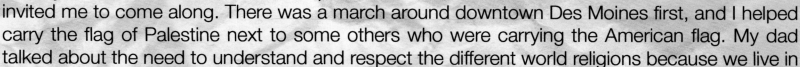

a global century. I hadn't planned any kind of speech. But I kept seeing all these ordinary people getting up on the platform to speak their minds. I got inspired. At first, my dad was nervous for me. I hadn't written anything down. "It's cool, Dad," I told him. "I can do this." All I did was say the things I believed in. At school, I had learned about Martin Luther King Jr. () I said he was a great man who started a great movement and we should finish it. After I spoke I felt proud, because I spoke for the hope of peace. My dad said he felt proud of me, too.

I didn't know anyone there, but they didn't seem like strangers. There were all these people, from tiny babies to great-grandparents, standing in the middle of that street downtown, all bundled up on a cold morning. They weren't

Peace Be Upon You

Muslims greet one another with the words "as-salaamu alaykum." In Arabic this means "peace be upon you," the peace achieved by faithful believers of Islam who submit to God's law. Many people might not realize a similar greeting was practiced by both Moses, the prophet of the Jewish faith, and by Jesus Christ. In the language of Judaism, Hebrew, one says "shalom aleichem," meaning "peace be upon you." Jesus, who spoke a dialect of Hebrew, taught Christians the same: "And as they thus speak, Jesus himself stood in the midst of them, and saith unto them, Peace be unto you." (Luke 24:36)

السلام عليكم

my family. But we all had something in common: we all hope for peace. (📷)

On that first morning in Gaza City, I had scouted out the mosque, the playground at the school, found the best bakery in the neighborhood and eaten one piece of mammal [ma-MOOL] and another piece of baklava [BOCK-la-va] before my brother was even out of bed. On our first morning in Des Moines, I got up early, too. I stood on the front porch of our new house between the big empty boxes we had unpacked and stored out there the night before. Real snow, thick as blankets, lay all around. (📷) The sky was pink. The frozen air pinched my ears and nose. I pulled on the first snow hat and mittens and snow boots I had ever owned (my mom always comes prepared) and looked up and down the long sidewalk. It seemed more like an icy, distant planet. No one was out. Even the birds in the bare trees sounded cold. School was supposed to start in two days. I had no idea where I was headed, but I couldn't wait to find out.

Leaving Laos

FROM LAOS TO DES MOINES, IOWA

DES MOINES, IA

LAOS

FACTS ABOUT LAOS

What is the capital city?	Vientiane, population: 200,000
How far is it from Iowa?	8,161 miles
What is a favorite afternoon snack?	Khao tom (steamed rice wrapped in leaves)
How many people are in the country?	6.8 million
What are common names?	BounSoung (boys), SomPhong (girls)

Eight-year-old Kong

sits in the back of a flat-bed truck. (📷) *Her parents, four sisters, and an uncle tuck in around her. The truck jolts forward and they grab onto metal poles strung with wires to keep from falling out. Kong looks back at their house, unaware that this is the last time she will see it. She holds a small bag of clothing and watches the village roll by. Stilt-houses follow one after another, their tin roofs gleaming in midday sun. Dirt paths lead to wells and outhouses. Gardens brim with guava, mangoes, and tamarind fruit. In the distance, giant palm trees fill the landscape and Kong can almost see her father's freshly planted field. Her mother sits next to her, clinging to a rice steamer and blankets. It seems strange taking a soup pot, but Kong keeps her questions to herself. Her older sisters wave to a friend as if they'll be back in a day or two. Suddenly their mother begins to cry.*

"I remember getting into a truck and my mother crying very badly." My parents didn't explain exactly what was going on. When it was time to leave, they handed each of us a sack of clothes and said that we were visiting our grandparents. We didn't pack much so it looked like we were coming back. There was a large group of Taidam families, like us, who planned to leave Laos after the Vietnam War. I had no idea we weren't coming back, or that if we had been caught leaving my father would have been arrested. We were one of the first groups to cross the Mekong River into Thailand. My father said that the first crossing was May 10, 1975. We crossed on May 11th during the day. At my grandparents' house, my mother told her family we were leaving. They chose to stay.

The Taidam Story

At the end of the Vietnam War, an estimated 175,000 people from Laos escaped to refugee camps in Thailand. They were joined by thousands of Southeast Asians, seeking freedom from Communist rule. Among the Lao people were 2,600 Taidam natives who had originated from China and Vietnam. They wished to find freedom and emigrate as one community—but no country or state was willing to take all of them at once. They had no place to go.

Then, in the fall of 1975, Governor Robert Ray invited the Taidam people to begin new lives in Iowa. By 1979, 3,500 refugees called Iowa home. The state became a leader in welcoming refugees from Laos, Cambodia, Thailand, and Vietnam. Today the vast majority of Taidam people live in Iowa, which they adopted as their homeland.

After our visit we took another truck taxi away from the village. Something wasn't right. The next thing I remember was getting off a small boat in Thailand, a place I had never been. A Buddhist temple stood at the top of a grassy hill next to a cemetery lot. They set up tents for a refugee camp. At eight years old, I didn't know what a refugee was or that I had become one. For my sisters and me, the cemetery became our playground. (📷) We slid down tomb stones and made up games. Our mother stood in line for a bundle of food each day. We made the best of it, not knowing where we were going or what it would be like.

Four months later I stepped aboard my first airplane. I remember eating a delicious apple on the flight to the United States. Sometimes that certain smell will trigger my memory.

Des Moines, IA 2010

Kong and two of her children, Jasmine and Kenny, walk through Iowa's State Historical Museum. They have come to see a special exhibit honoring Southeast Asian refugees who came to America. Photos and stories depict journeys of families who fled Vietnam, Laos, Cambodia, and Thailand. Some show triumphant arrivals of those who risked their lives to escape communism. Others show the tragedy of Vietnamese boat people who died while crossing the South China Sea without food or water. Captions fill in pieces of a story that Jasmine and Kenny are hearing for the first time. Jasmine stops and studies a photo taken inside refugee quarters at Camp Pendleton, California. The year is 1975. In the photo, fifteen or twenty families have staked out spaces separated by crates and piles of laundry. Bamboo mats line a dark wood floor where they sleep. (📷)

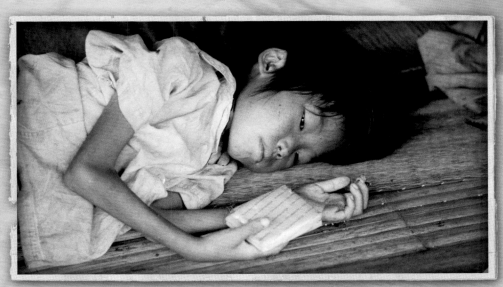

Finding Freedom

Kong's family left their village when Communist forces seized control of Laos. Since her father fought against the Communists, he was in danger of being captured by them. Under the new regime, Kong's family would lose their land and freedom. They left everything behind in search of a new homeland. Kong's parents did not tell her or her sisters about the plan so that they would not worry, and because they had to leave secretly. Her grandparents and other relatives joined them in the United States five years after they settled in Iowa.

Communist leader
Prince Souphanouvong

Kong points to the photo as memories of the refugee camps come back from when she was the same age as Kenny is now. There are no photos from her childhood in Laos or the camps.

"I had almost forgotten about Camp Pendleton," she says. "We stayed there for about a week before we went to Iowa. It was just like this picture—nothing between us except piles of whatever we had brought and mats on the floor."

Thaliand, 1979

Jasmine listens to her mom, seeing the reality of what she had to go through to get to the United States.

"I would definitely be scared not knowing where I was going," Jasmine says. "Growing up in one place and then leaving everything behind…having to make it look like we were coming back…I don't think I would have survived. I can't imagine being in a camp with no private space…with no choice," she says as Kenny looks at the photos.

Kong, Jasmine, and Kenny move to another display showing children at a camp in Thailand. They are outside with arms raised toward a stream of water pouring from a wooden bucket. (📷) Kenny asks about it and his mom explains that there were no showers.

"Your grandmother would gather us together and bathe us with a bucket of water. That's how we did it," Kong says. "People from other countries sent food, soap, and things for us to use. I remember learning some English before we left. Emnai (Kong's mother) had worked for an American family as a housekeeper in Laos. She taught your aunts and me some English phrases, like 'Yes,' 'No,' and 'Where's the bathroom?' I was in third grade when I started school in Iowa. I had a wonderful teacher, named Mr. Miller, who looked out for me. At recess, I took turns saying 'yes' or 'no' to whatever kids said. Most of them were nice, but I remember one or two who made fun of my accent. I was self-conscious and didn't want to read in front of them, but Mr.

Boat People

Vietnamese who escaped their homeland by sea in dangerous, overcrowded vessels were called boat people by the media. The term has been widely-used to describe these refugees.

Laos

Laos [sounds like house] is a land-locked country located in Southeast Asia. It is officially called: Lao People's Democratic Republic and is ruled by a communist government. Laos is 91,429 sq. miles (slightly larger than the state of Utah). Its terrain is mostly rugged and mountainous. The majority of its 6.8 million people live along the fertile plains of the Mekong and Irrawaddy River basins. Houses along the rivers are built on stilts to protect against flooding during the monsoon season from May through November. A dry season occurs from December through April. The climate is mostly tropical with an average annual temperature of 80 degrees Fahrenheit. Many Lao people work in industries such as: agriculture (growing rice, corn, coffee, sugarcane, and other crops), garment making, mining, and producing hydroelectric power from the major rivers.

Miller protected me. Whenever we had a picnic or field trip, he packed me a lunch."

Kenny and Jasmine look at their mom. She could have been one of the kids in these photos. How would that feel, blindly saying "yes" or "no" in a foreign language?

Jasmine, Kenny, and their middle sister, Melanie, are first-generation Iowans. Jasmine says that friends have asked a lot about where their parents are from.

"They're not being mean, they're just curious," she says. "When I was in fifth grade a friend of mine who is Hmong asked me lots of questions about where we're from. I told her I wasn't sure, so I asked my mom. It turned out that both of our families came from Laos. Most of us who were born in Iowa don't speak Hmong or Tai like our parents and grandparents, but we understand it. I hear it at home all the time."

"Hello" sounds like: CON-lah-kwah.
It also means "How are you?"
"I am fine" is: CON-sin-law.
"Good bye" is: BI-gom, with a soft "b" sound.

"After school we used to go to our grandparents' house for dinner. (📷) Now I usually have soccer or other high school activities, but we still go sometimes. It's very busy because our cousins and aunts come over, too. We call our grandmother Emnai [EM-ni] and our grandfather is Ita [I-dtah]. 'Em' means mother and 'I' means father. They speak Tai to us, but sometimes they'll use English to get our attention. Like, when we're watching TV and the volume is too loud. Emnai will yell in

Honoring Governor Ray

Taidam families commonly refer to Governor Ray as father of their people because he made it possible for them to begin new lives in Iowa. The Governor and Mrs. Ray inspired families, religious groups, and communities to help refugees settle in their new home state. The Robert D. Ray Asian gardens in Des Moines are a lasting symbol of this humanitarian effort. The Chinese Cultural Center of America, with its three-story Asian pavilion, also honors the significant contributions that Asian Americans, from many countries, have made to Iowa.

Governor Robert D. Ray

English to turn down the volume because she's getting a headache. Whenever we are there, she cooks for us. Emnai makes the best Tai food. Sausage, rice, and every kind of stir fry. One of my favorites is a dish called lop made with chicken, beef, fish, or any kind of meat, with onions and peppers over rice. My grandmother's cooking and language connect us to Laos."

Over the years, another connection for Jasmine and Melanie has been performing with a Taidam dance group. Practices begin in November and culminate in February at the Taidam New Year's festival. Jasmine and Melanie performed for about six years until their schedules filled with sports and music. Their teacher, Vilay, [VEE-li] continues the tradition with songs and choreography that tell the stories from the old country in Vietnam.

"It was a lot of fun," Jasmine says, "and not always easy. When I started I had to learn how to stick with the beat, and the hand motions were hard to get used to. We made paper flowers to hold during the dances. My favorite part was getting together and practicing with friends that we didn't usually see. We practiced Saturday afternoons and learned everything we could leading up to our New Year's."

Melanie describes the traditional outfits they wore for

final performances: "Ankle-length black skirts and Mandarin-style silk jackets with silver trim. We danced in bare feet, holding bright paper flowers with tiny silver bells, or scarves that accentuated our hand motions. One of my favorite performances was called Love at First Sight, which acted out the story of how Emnai and Ita might have met and dated as teenagers in Vietnam."

Emnai describes the scene in Tai as Kong translates: "Back then we had a stage in the middle of the village. Girls brought food to share and sewing and crafts to do, especially during a full moon. The boys serenaded us with two-string guitars, made from hollowed-out gourds, and bamboo pipes. We made a game of taking the ladder away so they couldn't get to us. But if the songs were good enough, we lowered the ladder and let the boys come up."

Taidam New Year at the Iowa State Fairgrounds is a long way from the stage in the middle of Emnai's village, yet some things haven't changed. Children and elders still beat dragon drums as families arrive for the celebration. Tot-cons fly through the air like miniature dragons. These colorful toys are hand-made from rice-filled bean bags and bright ribbons, as they always have been. Kids are eager to open money envelopes, and every generation dances and plays games. Fried rice, egg rolls, and sesame cakes crowd the tables for a pot-luck dinner. Food, flowers, and potted trees are reminiscent of the warmth and colors of Southeast Asia. Now Vietnamese, Hmong, and Tai mix with English from one generation to the next. Every family here has a story of a long journey.

For Kong's family, it begins in the back of a truck in a small Lao village. She had no idea that a trip to 'her grandparents' house' would lead her half-way around the world, or that her own children would grow up celebrating the Taidam New Year in a new homeland called Iowa.

What Thirteen Means

FROM ISRAEL TO IOWA

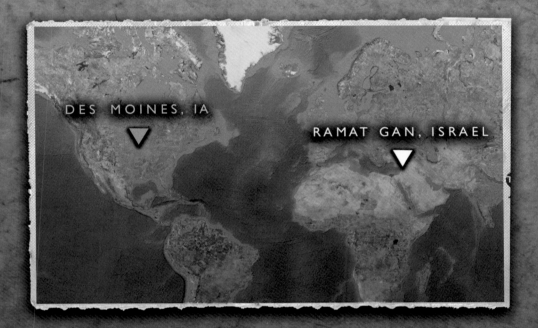

DES MOINES, IA

RAMAT GAN, ISRAEL

FACTS ABOUT ISRAEL

What is the capital city?
Jerusalem, population: 763,000

How far is it from Iowa?
6,425 miles

What is a favorite afternoon treat?
Krembo (biscuit with chocolate and meringue)

How many people are in the country?
7.6 million

What are common names?
Malachi and Elias (boys); Eden and Hala (girls)

It's a sunny Saturday evening

in late summer and young Ty Frankel is feeling very relieved. He has just experienced a day he will never forget. He's been preparing for this special day for many months, in some ways his whole life. Now the hard part is over. As the sun sets over West Des Moines, guests who have come from all over the country, some all the way from Israel, stream in ready to celebrate with Ty and his family. "You did awesome!" one of his cousins tells him. His aunt enfolds him in a big squeeze and tells him, "We are so proud of you." Some guests pause in the reception area to watch a computer screen slide show of special moments in Ty's life: Ty as a toddler with the same curly dark hair and brown eyes; Ty holding his baby brother; Ty shooting hoops wearing the golden-yellow jersey of his basketball team. This evening, dressed in a lavender shirt and dark slacks, Ty carries himself with a sense of pride in his accomplishment. Ty is turning thirteen, and today he became a bar mitzvah.

People think a bar mitzvah is something you have, like a ceremony, but it's actually something you are. If you're a Jewish boy, you automatically become a bar mitzvah—it means son of the commandments—when you turn thirteen. You don't have to have a ceremony to become one but it's tradition. Girls have one, too, called a bat mitzvah. ("Bat" means "daughter" in Hebrew).

If you do have a ceremony, it's a lot of work

to get ready. I studied with my cantor, a special Jewish teacher, and the rabbi (RAB-bye), our religious leader, for a half an hour a week for months. I had to learn a portion of the Torah, the Jewish holy book. I memorized it in Hebrew so I could recite it perfectly in front of my family and friends and the entire congregation. You don't really say it like a speech, it's more like singing or chanting, so you have to learn that, too. You're helping to lead the prayer service.

A lot of American kids have to learn Hebrew while they are learning their Torah portion. Hebrew is my first language, so it was easier for me. Still, the writing is ancient and written in tiny script. You do have to memorize it. It's fun knowing Hebrew because my little brother, Ben, and I use it kind of like code when we don't want other people to know what we're saying.

For us, being Jewish isn't really about being religious. Before I was born, my dad studied at Oxford, in Great Britain, and people sometimes treated him differently or said bad things about Jewish people. He said those experiences made him want to feel more connected to being Jewish, so he came to Israel and taught at the university, which is where he met my mom. I don't know any other Jewish kids at my school. For me, being Jewish is not as much what I believe or something I do; it's who I am. Once, a friend from school tried to convert me to Christianity. She was Christian and it was important to her. She invited me to a free pizza night with her church group.

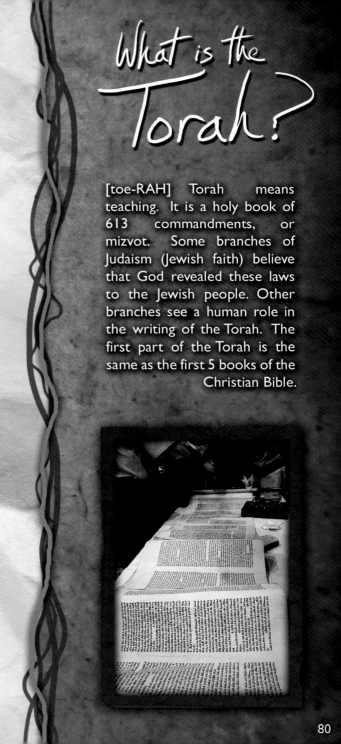

What is the Torah?

[toe-RAH] Torah means teaching. It is a holy book of 613 commandments, or mizvot. Some branches of Judaism (Jewish faith) believe that God revealed these laws to the Jewish people. Other branches see a human role in the writing of the Torah. The first part of the Torah is the same as the first 5 books of the Christian Bible.

What Eighteen Means

Thirteen is an important age for a Jewish boy, and 18 is an important number. The Hebrew word for life—"chai" (pronounced like "hi") is made up of the letter chet, which has the value of 8 and the letter yud, which has the value of 10. Together, they equal 18. At weddings, births, and bar/bat mitzvahs, $18 (or multiples of 18) is a typical gift, symbolizing life.

The Hebrew word "chai"

Then she wrote me a letter. She thought she was doing a good thing. But after that, we weren't friends because you have to respect people's beliefs. I respected hers but I felt like she wasn't able to respect mine.

We don't go to synagogue every week and we don't keep kosher [CO-sure] (see sidebar). My Saba (Grandpa) does. For me, it's more about the food my mom makes, my family, and the Hebrew language. My mom's an amazing cook. One of my favorite dishes is chameen, which is rice with meat, boiled eggs, matzoh balls (dumplings) (📷) and potatoes mixed with onions and spices. Traditionally, this dish takes 12 hours to cook, usually overnight. You bake it

on Friday and then eat it on Shabbat, the Sabbath day, when you aren't supposed to cook. Mom calls her version "chameen lite" because hers only cooks for three hours. For me, it's still the best.

Being Jewish is not something you can tell by looking at a person. My mom says she can always tell when someone is Israeli, though. I think I look Israeli, but someone told me I look Bosnian, so I guess people can't tell. To be honest, I prefer to think about basketball. I've been playing basketball since I was about five years old, and now I'm on an AAU (Amateur Athletic Union) basketball team called the Mid-city Mastiffs and my school's team, the Waukee Warriors. I hope to get a scholarship to play in college. After that, if I'm not good enough to play in the NBA, I hope to play in a European league for a while.

When you become a bar mitzvah and do all that studying, it doesn't mean you are done learning about the Torah or the Hebrew language once you turn thirteen. In a way it's just the beginning. Thirteen is the beginning of being responsible for yourself and your actions. You are no longer a child.

The ceremony is traditional, but actually it's not as big a deal in Israel as it is in the States. In Israel they didn't used to have the ceremony for girls as often—my mom did not have one—but here in the States it's as big a deal for girls as it is for boys, and much more formal. My Israeli uncle called and said he had bought a nice, new pair of jeans for the event. My mom had to remind him, "In America, you have to really

Zion

Zion is another name for Jerusalem, but has a much deeper meaning for many Jewish people, who regard the nation of Israel as their holy land and home. In 1948, "Zionists" established the State of Israel for Jewish people. But because this state was founded in the Arab territory of Palestine, unending conflict between Israelis and Palestinians has continued to the present day.

Dormition Church, resting on the modern "Mt. Zion"

Keeping Kosher

Keeping kosher (CO-sure] means following the portion of Jewish law that specifies how foods are to be prepared and eaten. Many of the laws have to do with health or just make good sense. For example, fruits and vegetables are kosher unless they have bugs on them! Many people are aware that Jewish people who keep kosher do not eat pork; this law does not have to do with health, however, and the Torah does not explain reasons for the laws.

A kosher restaurant.

dress up!" But that's okay. My family is a blend of American Jewish and Israeli Jewish, and I'm proud to be both.

Before my aliyah—that's when you are called to do your Torah reading--I put on my kippah (cap) and tallit (prayer shawl). My dad looked at me and said, "You'll do great." He got up and said a traditional prayer thanking God for removing the burden of responsibility for my actions. Until you turn thirteen, it's your parents' job to teach you to follow the mitzvahs. But when you become a bar mitzvah, that's your own responsibility. I looked out in the pews and saw my mom's big smile, any my brother Ben who looked nervous, too, and my baby brother, Eli, who made me smile because I could see him trying hard to be still, which he doesn't do that often. My good friends from school were there, and

some of the guys from my basketball team. And my Saba and Savta (my Israeli grandparents) who came from far away to be there, and my Grandpa and Grandpa and aunts and uncles and cousins. And in my heart was my beautiful baby sister, Mika Lee Frankel, who died when she was only two.

Everyone had faith in me that I was ready for this. But it's a little intimidating to stand in front of the holy scripture and give the aliyah. At first I went a little fast, and I thought the rabbi kind of raised his

חי	(khai = [to] live)
בר מצווה	(bar mitzvah)
בת מצווה	(bat mitzvah)
ישראל	(yisrael = Israel)
תורה	(Torah)
אמא	(ima = mother)
אבא	(abba = father)

his eyebrows at me. But then I started to relax. And the next thing I knew, the rabbi was singing and everyone was shouting "Mazel Tov!" [mozzleTOF] which means congratulations.

I also had to give a speech on what my Torah portion means to me. Here, the rabbi helped a lot. A lot of the mitzvahs don't seem relevant to today. For example, there is a rule about when you can muzzle your ox. I've never even seen an ox. But when you think about it, this rule explains kindness to animals. One of the rules I found most relevant to my life was that if you make a vow to the Lord your God, you must not put off fulfilling it. In other words, when you make a promise, stick to that promise.

After the bar mitzvah there is a big lunch for everyone at the synagogue. Then in the evening is the big celebration. My mom and dad had this for me at a nice hotel with a fancy dinner, music, and dancing—there's something for everyone because it's a party for the grown-ups, too. I got to sit at a center table with all my friends.

When we go home to Israel, it's so different. My mom says the minute she gets off the plane there, it feels like she's surrounded by family. It's so beautiful—after all, it's on the Mediterranean coast. The houses are all built of white stone. I was born in Israel, in Ramat Gan, which is near the city of Tel Aviv (📷 ▶). Jerusalem, the capitol, is one of my favorite cities. (📷 ▼) It's modern and ancient at the same time. You'll see people in the latest fashions and fancy hotels and clubs, and then you'll also see holy places where Jews or Christians or Muslims have worshipped since Biblical times. Iowa is so different. It's really green. And there's a lot more space, maybe too much in a way. People are packed together in Israel, and everyone walks, everyone's outside a lot. Once, we were staying with my aunt and uncle, and I was playing kick-the-can in the street with my cousins. It was a blast. We got in trouble for being too rowdy, but even that was kind of fun. Israelis can kind of get in your business, but they mean well. If you look tired or you're dressed funny, you're going to hear about it. But if you need help, they are there for you, always.

For me, Israel is so much more than what you hear in the news. It's where I was born, the place every Jewish person can call home. There is nowhere else they can go to experience this. When you're just a kid, your world is just your family and school and friends. When you turn thirteen, you have more understanding about the world. Nothing changes without it. One time I was playing basketball at the YMCA and was in and out of the gym where I left my

my backpack. When I was getting ready to go home I could not find my backpack anywhere. We discovered it had been stolen because my binder was later found dumped in the parking lot at the Dairy Queen. But now I see this as something that didn't just happen to me. It wasn't just my backpack being stolen. Where somebody steals something of yours it creates an atmosphere of distrust for everyone. I think you have to start with understanding.

The Beautiful Island

CARA AND JASMINE'S JOURNEY FROM TAIWAN

TAIWAN

DES MOINES, IA

FACTS ABOUT TAIWAN

What is the capital city?	Taipei, population: 2.6 million
How far is it from Iowa?	7,324 miles
What is a favorite afternoon snack?	Suncake
How many people are in the country?	23 million
What are examples of Chinese names?	Girls: Lǐm Méi, Boys: Tǎn Sōng

Red and white

baskets hover across a school field. Cara and her classmates chase after them, tossing beanbags into the air. Someone makes a shot and Cara's team jumps up and down. A carrier empties a basket from its bamboo pole and the fun begins again. Kids scramble to even the score. Classmates cheer. Their bright matching t-shirts line a track where races begin next. Out on the field another carrier passes a white basket to her teammate. Beanbags fly in every direction. Players scoop them up for one last shot. A whistle blows and new teams take their turn in the aerial beanbag toss. Behind them, Shuan Foung (Double Peak) Mountain rises up against an endless spring sky—a perfect backdrop for this magical day that happens once a year at Shuan Foung Elementary. (📷) No classes today. It's Marathon Day!

Cara Liu remembers this as one of the best days of the year as a fourth-grader in Taipei.

Everyone loved Marathon Day. It was our time to have fun. We didn't wear school uniforms, just shorts and t-shirts. Instead of a real marathon we ran races and played games all afternoon. Each class put on marching events and performances. I remember playing instruments we made from plastic bottles. Some kids acted out funny skits, but my favorite event was the beanbag game. To make it super-challenging someone from each team carried their basket around the field, dodging every shot. By the end of the day we all had a chance to play. Older kids helped younger ones. Teachers, students, and families spread blankets on the field for lunch and prizes. It was something we looked forward to every year.

My mom and dad owned a bakery in Hsin Tien city. (📷) They worked long hours. Sometimes they couldn't make it to school events, but then they would surprise me and bring my younger sister, Jasmine, with boxes from the bakery. The two of us would pass out Mom's cakes and cookies at the end of the races. Everyone loved them.

Regular days at school were nothing like Marathon Day. In Taiwan we spoke Mandarin, a form

of Chinese, and went to school six days a week: Monday through Friday, plus a half day on Saturday. Our school was named Shuan Foung, which means Double Mountain, after the huge twin peaks outside our classrooms. We wore black plaid skirts, or dark pants for the boys, with white shirts. We had lots of homework. I remember staying up late sometimes to get it done, even in second grade. Our teachers were good but also very strict. If we did something wrong, or our nails weren't trimmed, teachers would hit our hands with a ruler. If you pulled your hand away you would get hit twice. My fourth grade teacher taught all of our subjects. After morning lessons we went outside to play and run around the track with the mountain right there. Kids brought lunch to school. Mom sent rice cakes and sometimes a surprise from the bakery. She always remembered to pack my cup and toothbrush because we brushed our teeth each day after recess.

In class we learned to read and write Chinese characters. It's different from English where there's an alphabet to sound out words. With Chinese there is no alphabet. Speaking Mandarin and writing it are like two totally separate languages. For writing, each word has its own symbol. We had to memorize them. It takes a lot of practice. In class we studied their meanings and wrote them over and over. When Jasmine and I left Taiwan we still had a lot of characters to learn. Here are some examples:

人 man   大 big   小 small   天 sky

馬 horse   龍 dragon   田 farm   愛 love

Taiwan

Taiwan is located in the South China Sea off the coast of China. It is a small island, (13,892 sq. miles) relative to its large population of 23 million people. For comparison, Taiwan has about 1,894 people per square mile, while Iowa has 52.4 people per square mile. Across the U.S. the average is 84.

The name Taiwan means "terraced bay" in Chinese. It is often referred to as "Illa Formosa," which means "beautiful island" because of its rich forests, jagged mountain ranges, and rocky coastlines. It has a subtropical climate, with hot, humid summers and mild winters. During winter, snow falls atop the highest mountain peaks, more than 10,000 feet above sea level.

Taiwan and China are both known around the world for making high tech products, such as computers.

Spoken Chinese Language (Yu)

Chinese is the most widely spoken language in the world, with about one-fifth of all people speaking some form of Chinese as their native language. There are seven major branches of spoken Chinese, including: Mandarin, Wu, Cantonese, Min, Jin, Xiang, and Hakka. While these spoken languages differ widely, they share one written form of Chinese.

For example, the spoken word for man is "ren" in Mandarin, "ning" in Wu, and "yen" in Cantonese, but the written symbol stays the same: 人.

Character for "Buddha"

At the end of the school day everyone had a special job, like sweeping the floor, organizing books, or cleaning desks for the next day. Each class worked as a team.

After school Mom and Dad were busy at the bakery, so Jasmine and I entertained each other. After homework we would play games and see our friends. At night our family slept on a long wooden platform bed in our apartment behind the bakery. Mom and Dad were still working when Jasmine and I would fall asleep, and in the morning they were taking things out of the oven before we woke up.

I was in fourth grade and Jasmine in first when our parents told us we were moving to the United States. Our dad was going to work for a family company that our uncle had started in Iowa. It was hard to leave our friends and school. I remember the day we left. Some of them surprised us at the airport. It meant a lot to see them, but it was sad to say goodbye. My best friend gave me a Panda bear that holds Taiwanese coins, which I still keep.

On the plane I was excited and scared. When I got to Iowa I wanted to go back home to Taipei. On the first day of school, my teacher introduced me at the front of the class. I had seen pictures of American kids, but to see so many of them . . . I felt like I stood out from everyone else. I did not speak English except for a few A, B, C's. By far, the hardest part about coming here was not knowing the language. Kids treated me differently. At first, I didn't know when someone made fun of me, but my ears burned. As I learned English, my words sounded different. It was hard. In the beginning, I had a few Asian friends, and then I met more friends. One of them came here from Bosnia, so she understands what it's like to move to a different country with a different language. Some days it's still hard, but when you have close friends it makes a big difference. Now it feels like home is here.

For Jasmine, starting in first grade was a lot easier. Younger kids don't notice the way you look and your differences as much as older kids do. We both took ESL (English as a Second Language) classes for a while. After two years we didn't need ESL. Then it was the opposite: knowing how to write and speak English and forgetting our Chinese. At school we speak English, but at home we mix English with Mandarin. Our grandparents live with us and speak Mandarin, so we practice with them. Grandma is "Nai-Nai" [nī- nī] and Grandpa is "Ye-Ye." [yā-yā] They love to hear what we are doing at school. We tell them about our classes, art, and playing flute. For a while we tried to take Chinese after school, but it was so hard to get our regular homework done. We wanted to learn more Chinese and our parents worried that we would forget our language, culture, and our

Written Chinese Language (Wen)

Calligraphy, the art of writing Chinese characters, is honored and passed from one generation to the next. There are about 3,000 characters for the words in every-day Chinese language and at least 60,000 in all. Written Chinese is an open-ended system, which means that there is no limit to the number of characters. Each character symbolizes one syllable or idea in the meaning of a word.

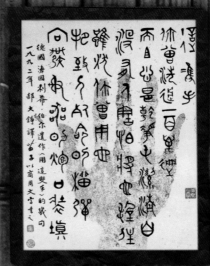

Buddhist religion, which we practice at home with evening prayers.

When I was ready to start high school my mom came up with the idea of sending me to a school in California—an international school to continue my Chinese education and Buddhist teachings. I had my friends, and my whole schedule for high school was set here in Iowa. I did not want to leave and have to start all over again in a new place. I cried and told my mom she could not do this to me. But she said how wonderful the school was in a place called the City

of Ten Thousand Buddhas, a couple hours from San Francisco. She had been there and thought it would be a great experience for me. Jasmine and I went to a summer camp there to try it out. I liked it, but I still wasn't sure. Jasmine was the one who really wanted to go there, so we both went. I started ninth grade and Jasmine began in sixth. It's a different experience, going away to an all girls' school. Each class is small. We're a very close group. Now Jasmine and I love it there just as much as being home.

City of Ten Thousand Buddhas, California

Cara and Jasmine walk with friends toward the Jeweled Hall of Ten Thousand Buddhas. (📷) Their black silky robes shift in the breeze as they join Buddhist monks, nuns, and worshipers of many religions. Peacocks fan their feathers, matching the colorful murals painted on the building. An image of King Virupaksha, King of the West, stares down at them, followed by paintings of the three other kings of the East, South, and North. Students whisper at the end of the line and fall silent when they reach the entrance. Inside, the smell of incense fills the air. Women and girls take their place on the right side as men and boys sit on the left, across a wide aisle. Hundreds of golden cushions form neat rows leading to an altar. This is the only time students from the boys' and girls' schools see each other. As the evening service begins, it is no time to socialize.

CTTB

The City of Ten Thousand Buddhas (CTTB) at Wonderful Enlightenment Mountain is an international Buddhist community established in 1976 as a sanctuary for followers of all the world's religions.

Schools

Instilling Goodness Elementary School (kindergarten through eighth grade) and Developing Virtue Secondary School, (grades 9-12), focus on fundamental human values in addition to traditional academics.

A tower near the temple.

Buddhism

Buddhism is one of the great world religions. It began in India about 2500 years ago, based on the teachings of Buddha. Among other beliefs, Buddhists emphasize doing good for others and not becoming too attached to material things. Today there are an estimated 360 million Buddhists worldwide, with more than 1 million living in the United States.

A common Buddha statue

Inside the Buddha Hall is like a gymnasium with rows and rows of cushions for us to bow on. I didn't expect anything like it when I first walked in—the way the air smells, and golden Buddhas everywhere. There really are 10,000, even more. Each Buddha is about ten inches tall and was made by Venerable Master Hua who founded our schools. He made two every night, from molds of earth and clay, and painted every single one of them gold. He worked for several years until he finished all 10,000. Enormous Buddhas, about

three or four times as tall as a regular person, are at the front and back of the hall. Students enter the evening service wearing the same black robes, all of us equal. Up front monks and nuns in brown or gray robes lead the service. They wear their robes all the time, but we only wear ours for worship. The boys sit on the opposite side and we almost never talk with them. The Abbott stands in the aisle between us, wearing red and gold robes. Only he can wear those colors since he's the leader of the monks and nuns. The opening chant is always the same, honoring the Buddhas with Incense Praise. A monk starts chanting and we follow along in the Book of 10,000 Buddhas. It's a very important book of Buddhist teachings written in Chinese and English. We trade off reading in each language every other night. Sometimes they're easier to memorize in Chinese because they were written in verse, like poetry.

After the evening service we go back to our dorm and do homework and hang out. On Fridays we look forward to the weekend. One of the best things about living at school is that we're all girls and we're really, really close, especially in the dorm. We can be ourselves. No one has to put on makeup or dress special. We go to each other's rooms, which are in one open space. I feel like my classmates are true friends who care about me. We help each other with volunteer work in the City of Ten Thousand Buddhas. We try to keep our school neat because we're the ones who clean it. Everyone has duties that change each month. No one wants wake-up duty because that means getting everyone up at 6 AM for breakfast.

Classes go from 8:00 AM to 4:00 PM. Jasmine and I take regular classes, like math, science, and English, plus Chinese and virtue studies, which are part of Buddhist learning. One of the best parts about school here is that they don't only care about academics, but our personal well-being and caring for others.

One of Jasmine's and my favorite activities in the community is the Buddha's Birthday, or bathing day. (📷) It represents when the Buddhas were born. Every spring

hundreds of people come to wash the golden Buddhas made especially for the event. We make flower wreaths and hang decorations around campus. Before the celebration we set up stations outside with bowls of pure water. Jasmine and I, and all of our friends, draw chalk arrows on the sidewalks, and show visitors where to go. In the morning we have a service in the great hall. Afterward everyone comes outside to bathe the Buddhas. We kneel down on a pillow in front of a Buddha statue, then pour water from a long ladle over the Buddha's shoulders—not over the head, because that is considered disrespectful. When we're finished pouring the water, we stand up and do a half bow to the Buddha.

On most Saturdays we hang out and play around. The school gives out times to go on field trips. We've been to the ocean a few times. It's really cool—the blue Pacific and beaches with a million little things in the sand. Sometimes we hike and see animals, like donkeys, deer, and sheep, and the peacocks around our school. Most of our food is grown right here, all vegetarian. We are surrounded by woods and hills, like Enlightenment Mountain. Our school is a beautiful place. A second home for us.

Jasmine and I are best friends. We have never been separated—from Taiwan, to Iowa, to California. I don't know what I would do without her, but I am glad we're together.

Perry Las Posadas

FROM MEXICO TO IOWA

PERRY, IA

GUADALAJARA, MEXICO

FACTS ABOUT MEXICO

What is the capital city?	Mexico City, population: 8.8 million
How far is it from Iowa?	1,559 miles
What is a favorite afternoon treat?	*Bunuelos*
How many people are in the country?	112.3 million
What are the most common names?	Miguel and Diego (boys); Maria and Valeria (girls)

Samantha walks down the steps

of Saint Patrick's Church on a clear December night. She drapes a silky blue shawl over her head and pulls it close against the cold. Her white dress brushes the sidewalk. A young man named Alex touches her arm and walks beside her. His clothing is similar, a head dress and robe reminiscent of biblical times. (📷) *Men, women, and children follow them into town. Some wear costumes, like Samantha and Alex's, some are in jeans and winter coats.*

"Hola, Maria y Jose," or, "Hello, Mary and Joseph," they say. The two smile and wish everyone "Feliz Navidad!" or "Merry Christmas!" Tonight is Las Posadas. The Spanish tradition reenacts the Bible story of Mary and Joseph as they searched for shelter on the night before Jesus was born. In Perry, Iowa the celebration is a mix of Hispanic and American families. They sing the scenes of Mary and Joseph as they stop at storefronts along Main Street. Each time they knock on a door, half of the crowd goes inside while Samantha, Alex and the others are left out in the cold- just as Mary and Joseph were on the first Christmas Eve. In the Bible there was no room for them at the inn, but tonight Samantha and Alex lead the way to a celebration where everyone enjoys Mexican food and music. The crowd grows with the strumming of guitars, and hymns sung in Spanish and English. (📷) *Samantha and her sisters sing both versions with ease. They speak the language of their mother, Lourdes, from Mexico, and their father, Tony, from Iowa. Yet*

Las Posadas

Las Posadas is the Spanish word for "The Inns" or "The Shelters." In Mexico and other Latin American countries it is a social and religious celebration commemorating the difficult journey of Mary and Joseph from Nazareth to Bethlehem before Jesus was born.

Traditionally, Las Posadas is a nine-day celebration. The idea began in the sixteenth century when Saint Ignatius Loyola used a popular festival of the Aztec Sun God to teach about the birth of Christ. He wanted to replace the nine-day Aztec holiday with a Christian celebration. Las Posadas began as nine days of prayer, but over many years the festivities moved from churches out into Hispanic homes and communities around the world.

shifting between Spanish and English wasn't always easy. Samantha remembers a time when her place between cultures resembled the passage of Mary and Joseph, searching for a place to stay.

When I was little, I stayed home speaking Spanish with my mom all day, Samantha says. My parents both wanted me to speak Spanish first, growing up in Iowa. Sometimes I cried when Dad got home from work because I couldn't understand him. He and Mom seemed to understand each other perfectly, even though they spoke different languages, but for me it was hard. The first day of kindergarten I didn't know what my teachers were saying. I pretended to be sick so I wouldn't have to go. At nap time I was sent out of the

Mexico

Mexico, officially known as the United Mexican States, (Estados Unidos Mexicanos), has more Spanish-speaking people than any other country in the world. It is nearly three times the size of Texas, (760,601 square miles), with a population of approximately 111 million. Most Mexicans, (70%), live in urban areas around cities such as Mexico City and Guadalajara. Mexico has 31 states and a federal district where Mexico City, the capital, is located.

Tourism is an important industry with Mexico's long coastlines and many cultural attractions. (📷) Along the Gulf of Mexico the weather is hotter and more humid than in the higher elevations of central Mexico with plateaus, desert areas, and mountains that reach up to 18,000 feet.

room to a separate ELL (English Language Learner) class with other Hispanic kids. It upset me, having to leave every day. Once I knew both languages things changed. I never really noticed. It just happened. Now I speak Spanish or English depending on the situation. My younger sisters and I help translate at school and other places. Sarah skips recess to help kids from Mexico learn English. Sabrina translates teachers' instructions in music, art, and gym class. One time, on our way to school, a mom lost her child. "Have you seen my son?" she asked the crossing guard in Spanish. The guard didn't understand her and she got really upset. Sabrina translated for them, and we found the kid a few minutes later. Or, at the grocery store, a Hispanic lady in front of us didn't know how much she needed to pay, so we helped her out. We're used to it.

Now, going into high school, some kids speak both languages. Teachers don't always like kids speaking Spanish in class. Once I was sitting toward the back and some boys started swearing in Spanish. The teacher didn't know what they were saying. All of a sudden I spoke their language. They were shocked that I understood everything they had said. I told them to stop talking like that, to have some respect. They didn't talk like that again.

My friends think it's cool that my mom is from Mexico and my dad is from Iowa. But sometimes people are surprised when I speak Spanish, because I don't look Hispanic. I'm American and Mexican. Some kids think you have to be in one group or the other, but my friends are both. For me it's not about whether you're white or Hispanic but what you're into. We hang out at our house after school. Everyone loves my mom and her Mexican food (📷), and Mom loves having them over. It's different from where she grew up. We do a lot of things she was never allowed to do. My sisters and I decorate our rooms. We play sports and do activities with

boys and girls. Mom grew up with six sisters and a brother. Girls went to separate schools and were told that their role was to clean the house and cook. In Guadalajara, the mother ruled the house. Mom still rules our house, but she  wants us to have choices. I run track, and play golf, and volleyball. Everyone hears her at volleyball games, cheering loudly in Spanish: "Corrale! tu Puedes!" (Go! You can do it!)

This December I turn fifteen. Many Hispanic girls have Quinceañeras, [keen-sen-NYAIR-ah], to celebrate. My parents said it's my choice, and I decided to have one. I want my mom to be very involved because she never had a

Quinceañera

Quinceañera, [keen-se-NYAIR-ah], means fifteen (quince) years (anara). In many Hispanic cultures a Quinceañera is a coming of age celebration on a girl's fifteenth birthday. The term refers to both the event and the honoree. It typically begins with a religious ceremony to recognize the girl's transition from child to young woman. After church a grand celebration is held. The Quinceañera chooses key elements of her celebration, much like a bride chooses for her wedding, including: her dress, honor court, and cake. A Quinceañera, like the one Samantha will have, reflects the personal and cultural style of each young lady, regardless of the size of the celebration.

Celebrating 15 years

Quinceañera. This is for her, too. It will be a different kind of 'Quince.' Sometimes they're so big, people you don't even know start showing up. Mine will be with close friends. For my attendants I'm having five girls and five guys. They think it's cool that I'm having a Quinceañera and that they'll be in it. Most of them have never been to one. One of the guys, who's a good friend of mine, lives on a farm. When I first met him, he didn't know I was Hispanic. The first time he came to our house I was really worried that he would think it was weird, seeing me speaking Spanish with my mom. But she made him feel right at home, like she does with everyone.

When my grandfather visited for a month it was different. He lives in the old Mexican way of doing things. Abuelito (grandpa) expected Mom to make all of his meals. He doesn't approve of her working outside the home. When Dad cooks and cleans up, Abuelito says Mom should be doing this. At his house it's a different world. In Guadalajara, they don't have many cars. Everyone walks or takes the bus. When we visited, we walked to markets to get bread, milk, and vegetables for each meal because they don't have refrigerators and freezers like we do.

There's a bakery right next to Abuelito's house. We had warm bread for breakfast every morning. The best part was the cajeta, (ca-HAY-tah), spread on top like caramel. When Abuelito came to Iowa, he brought us more. Sabrina, Sarah, and I had fun with him when he was here, but I wondered what he thought of us doing things that my mom and her sisters couldn't do when they were kids.

Our house is a blend of Iowa and Mexico—from how we talk, to what we eat, and the way things look. Mom loves to decorate. Our dining room table is set with pretty dishes, and everything's neat like she would have it in Mexico. Depending on who's cooking, it might be mac-and-cheese with homemade enchiladas, or maybe tuna fish mixed with sour cream, onions, and tomatoes. Even our religion is a blend of Mom, who's Catholic, and Dad, who's not as religious but still goes to church with us sometimes. Mom brought back the painting in our front hall from Guadalajara, and a display case filled with her special things.

As Samantha translates, her mom explains each item in her collection:

I am a very religious person, Lourdes says, opening the glass door of a curio cabinet without a speck of dust. These are the things I grew up with. They help protect our family and keep us happy and well, she says. This doll represents Baby Jesus. When I was a girl in Mexico, we didn't have Santa Claus. At Christmas we asked Jesus for gifts. Instead of hanging stockings, we left one of our shoes beside him. On Christmas morning we each had two small gifts hidden inside. Lourdes shows off a few more items and pauses before a statuette of a lady dressed in blue and

Perry, Iowa is located 25 miles northwest of Iowa's capital city of Des Moines. Like many central Iowa towns, it represents a crossroads between the state's vast agricultural community and the more urban lifestyle in Des Moines.

Along with farmers' markets, arts, and cultural events, Perry is known for its special blend of European and Hispanic culture. Nearly 25% of Perry's 7,633 residents consider themselves Hispanic. (compared to 12%, nationally, and about 3% across Iowa). In Perry Public Schools the Hispanic influence is even greater with 46% of students from Hispanic families. Events like Las Posadas highlight the sharing of cultural traditions.

Our Lady of Guadalupe

In 1531, Our Lady of Guadalupe appeared to a poor Indian farmer named Juan Diego. She said that she was the Mother of God and wished for a church where she could show her love to the people. Guadalupe told Juan Diego to ask the Spanish Bishop to build this church, but Juan could not convince him. The Bishop wanted proof that the Lady from Heaven had appeared. So, Guadalupe sent Juan with roses that had bloomed from the rocky hillside. She arranged them in his tilma, or cloak. When Juan opened his tilma with the flowers, the Bishop and everyone were awed by the painting of the Virgin Guadalupe that miraculously appeared in the fabric. Today the painting remains in perfect condition. Millions of people visit the Basilica, "La Villa de Guadalupe," in the north of Mexico City, to see it and pray to Our Lady of Guadalupe.

rose-colored robes, edged in gold. This is Guadalupe, Lourdes says with pride. She motions her daughters to help tell the legend of Mexico's Patron Saint. They shift easily between languages as the sacred story unfolds. Our Lady of Guadalupe is the protector of all Hispanic people, Samantha says. (📷) A long time ago she appeared to a poor Aztec farmer, named Juan Diego, with a message for the Spanish Bishop to build a church where she was standing. . .

As Samantha and her sisters explain, one of Guadalupe's greatest blessings is the blending of cultures. It began when Aztec Indians and Spaniards came together in a country known today as Mexico. (📷) Her blessing continues in Samantha's family and community where Hispanic and American cultures live together every day. In December the town of Perry will celebrate Las Posadas once again, and all will be welcomed at the inn.

About CultureAll
EXPERIENCE A WORLD OF DIFFERENCE

CultureAll is an Iowa-based non-profit organization creating cultural experiences that strengthen understanding and appreciation in our daily lives. Programs include Culture in the Classroom, Multicultural Days, Photo Ethnography, Fast-Track Diplomats and Teacher Training. Please visit them on the web at www.cultureall.org.

About ICIU
IOWA COUNCIL FOR INTERNATIONAL UNDERSTANDING

The Iowa Council for International Understanding (ICIU) was formed in 1938 to assist immigrants fleeing the war in Europe. ICIU continues its outreach to immigrants and refugees by connecting them with the resources they will need to live, work, and raise a family in Iowa. Their mission is to grow cultural respect around the world and at home, one person at a time. You can visit them online at www.iciu.org.

Credits

WRITTEN BY

Kay Fenton Smith and Carol Roh Spaulding

PRODUCED BY

Danny Heggen, of Shrieking Tree

ART DESIGN / PHOTO EDITOR

Justin Norman, of Shrieking Tree

ORIGINAL PHOTOGRAPHY

Phillip Harder and Justin Norman

PROJECT INTERNS

Merle Domer and Mikaela Jorgensen

PUBLISHED BY

Shrieking Tree
www.shriekingtree.com

FRONT COVER

"African Sunrise" by Teresa Allen
"Child and Bridge" by Phillip Harder

ACKNOWLEDGEMENTS

"Airplane" by Michael Osmenda (i)
"Foggy Bridge" by Mike Burns (i)

FOREWORD

"Young Ray and Refugees" courtesy Robert D. Ray (iii)

AUTHORS' NOTE

"Windmills of Walnut" by Ryan Craney (v)

STORIES

"Midwestern Airplane" by Wesley Norman (vi)
"Center Street Bridge Grand Opening" by Phil Roeder (vi)
"Map Texture" by Brenda Clarke (vi)

ZAKERY'S BRIDGE

"Mostar Bridge" by Francesco Vona (1)
"Mostar to Des Moines Map" by TerraMetrics / NASA (2)
"Damaged Library Card" by Justin Norman (2)
"Zakery by the Framed Bridge" by Terry J. Stober (3)
"Neretva" by Mark McEnery (4)
"Sarajevo Market" by Marella Luca (5)
"Mostar Bombed Building" by Chris McLemore (5)
"Bridge Blueprints" by HodakMoment (6)
"Bosnia & Herzegovina Map" by Justin Norman (7)
"Bosnian Text" by Justin Norman (7)
"Mostar Bridge" by Alistair Young (8)
"Technique (Diver)" by Jordan Wooley (8)
"Video Games" by Phillip Harder (9)
"Bosnia Cello" by Mikhail Evstafiev (10)
"Destroyed Bridge" courtesy anonymous (10)
"Ferry-boat" by Katarina Stefanovic (11)
"Bosnian Currency" by Justin Norman (12)
"Bosnian Soccer" by Péter Muzslay (13)
"Go Velez!" by Justin Norman (13)
"Bosnian Soccer 2" by Péter Muzslay (13)
"Don't Forget" by Craig Jakich (14)

SUMMERS IN SAGAR

"Jaisalmer" by Sabamonin (15)
"Des Moines to Sagar Map" by TerraMetrics / NASA (16)
"Sand and Stone Texture" by Jody Trappe (16)
"Shriya and Appaji" by Dinesh Rao (17)
"Rickshaws" by Marcus J. Roberts [http://bgerk.com] (18)
"Hindu Altar" by Justin Norman (19)
"Anika's Bindi" by Justin Norman (20)
"Sunset Bridge" by J.L. Schnabel (21)
"Bangles" by Kamakshi Sachidanandam * (22)
"Shriya's Dance" by Justin Norman (22)

"Rangoli" by Anne "Pondspider" Roberts * (23)
"Blue City" by Sabamonin (24)

WHERE THE FLOWERS ARE ◢▬

"Long-horned Cattle" by Wild Images [wildimages.tv] (25)
"Mayenthon to Des Moines Map" by TerraMetrics / NASA (26)
"Brown Cloth" by Justin Norman (26)
"Cattle in the River" by Helen Lynn (27)
"D is for Dau" by Justin Norman (28)
"Dinka Youth" by David Blume [daveblumenkrantz.com] (29)
"Children's Play" by Maria Giurova (30)
"Lion" by Jelle Prins * (31)
"Siblings" by David Blume (31)
"Peeking Hyena" by Mike Richardson (32)
"Minding the Cattle" by (33)
"A Question of Taste (Water Bucket)" by Rhoda Idoniboye (34)
"Fat Goat" by Martin Wilson (35)
"Refugee Camp" by (35)
"Dao's Family" courtesy his family (36)
"Dinka Jump Contest" by Carlo Grossi (37)
"Manute Bol" by Associated Press (37)
"Dinka Girls" by David Blume [daveblumenkrantz.com] (38)
"Fishing with Nets" by Hassan Elhassan (38)
"Two Dinka Youths" by David Blume [daveblumenkrantz.com] (39)
"Kurmuk, Blue Nile, Sudan" by Arsenie Coseac [http://eos.io] (40)

LITTLE DUTCH GIRL ▬

"Jenny Reuling" by Phillip Harder (41)
"The Netherlands to Des Moines Map" by TerraMetrics / NASA (42)
"Hay Texture" by Scott Shatto * (42)
"Jenny on the Tractor" by Phillip Harder (43)
"Ryanna with Cat" by Justin Norman (44)
"Nicklaus" by Justin Norman (44)
"Deltawerken" by Martin Terber * (44)
"Locked Up Cows" by Justin Norman (45)
"Nicklaus and Pumpkin" by Phillip Harder (46)
"Sinterklaas" by Lodewijk Borsboom * (46)
"Dutch Clogs" by Phillip Harder (47)
"Cows" by Phillip Harder (47)
"Dutch Doughnuts" by Misty Bushell (48)

"Hans Brinker Harlingen" by Roel Wijnants * (49)
"Husky Clouds Hover O'er the Fields" by Justin Norman (50)

▬ DREMALI STREET

"Gazing Over Gaza" by Suhair Karam / IRIN * (51)
"Gaza to Des Moines Map" by TerraMetrics / NASA (52)
"Rashad Dremali" courtesy his family (53)
"Drinking the Gaza" by White Ant (54)
"Injured Infant" by Zoriah Miller (55)
"Rockets" by Amid Farshad Ebrahimi * (55)
"Free Gaza" by Edo Medicks * (55)
"Boy Beside Lockers" by John Steven Fernandez * (56)
"Qur'an" by Ramy Alaa * (57)
"Dome of the Rock" by Peter Mulligan (58)
"Mecca" by Ammar Abd Rabbo * (58)
"Praying Muslim" by Jano Fistialli * (59)
"Boy Holding Shell" by Andreas H. Lunde * (59)
"Children Running Through Rubble" by anonymous (59)
"Bowing Muslims" by anonymous (60)
"Ramadan Meal" by Reway2007 (61)
"Martin Luther King, Jr." by Dick DeMarsico (62)
"Give Peace a Chance" by Jeff Gitchel (62)
"Hands Linked" by Jeff Gitchel [http://turtlemoon.org] (63)
"Fog and Ice" by Louis (CR Artist) (64)

▬ LEAVING LAOS

"Laotian Field" by Rick Horne (65)
"Laos to Des Moines Map" by TerraMetrics / NASA (66)
"Mango" by Geanina Bechea (66)
"Kong's Family" by Kay Fenton Smith (67)
"Dusty Road to Mandalay" by Lite Choices (68)
"Chinese Cemetery, Kanchanburi" by Ross Thomson * (69)
"Girl on Bamboo" by Corbis Images (70)
"Prince Souphanouvong" painting photographed by Nick Hubbard (70)
"Girl with Bucket" courtesy of Robert D. Ray (71)
"A Fun Shower" by Fred Blandford (72)
"Vietnamese Boat People" by Phil Eggman * (72)
"Boat People Family" by Felimon Barbante [National Archives] * (72)
"Laos Map" by Justin Norman (73)
"Fried Rice" by Alpha Lau [flickr.com/avlxyz] (74)

"Robert D. Ray and Child" by Kay Fenton Smith (75)
"Drumming Monks" by Bob Bowden (76)

WHAT THIRTEEN MEANS

"Ramat Gan" by Amir Yalon (77)
"Ramat Gan to Des Moines Map" by TerraMetrics / NASA (78)
"Speckles" by Martha Perez [flickr.com/marthamadnesspdx] (78)
"Ty's Bar Mitzvah" by Stephen Mendenhall (79)
"Nehar Shalom Community Synagogue Torah" by Steve Garfield (80)
"Gold Letters" by Howard Sandler (81)
"Matzoh Balls" by Megabeth [http://megabeth.net] (81)
"Dormition Church" by Andrew Bossi * (82)
"Kosher Pizza" by Jessica Spengler * (82)
"Ty and Friend" by Justin Norman (83)
"Old and New Jerusalem" by Brian Negin (85)
"Tel Aviv" by anonymous (86)

THE BEAUTIFUL ISLAND

"Taipei" by Daniel M. Shih (87)
"Taipei to Des Moines Map" by TerraMetrics / NASA (88)
"Old Wood Room" by Caesart (88)
"Cara and Jasmine" by Kay Fenton Smith (89)
"Shuan Foung Mountain and School" by anonymous (90)
"Bakery Sweets" by Justin Norman (91)
"Chinese on Rusty Background" by Photobank (93)
"Airplane" by Tony Lin (93)
"Chinese Calligraphy Today" by Maryellen McFadden (94)
"Inside 10,000 Buddhas Monastery" by Sarah Grimwood (95)
"Ten Thousand Buddhas Tower" by Sarah Grimwood (96)
"The Laughing and Lucky Buddha" by William Cho (97)
"Dark-Robed Monks" by Johnny Barker (97)
"Cara and Jasmine at School" by Kay Fenton Smith (98)
"Buddha Bathing" by Jamie Carter (98)
"Peacock" by Andrea Rapisarda [http://rapis60.redbubble.com] (99)
"Cara and Jasmine Pond" by Tony Liu (99)
"Taipei Sunset" by Jennifer Kecl * (100)

PERRY LAS POSADAS

"Guadalajara Houses" by M. Peinado * (101)
"Guadalajara to Des Moines Map" by TerraMetrics / NASA (102)

"Wall Texture" by David Gunter * (102)
"Mary and Joseph" by Kay Fenton Smith (103)
"Carolers" by Rachel Sardell (104)
"Boats and Clouds" by Lorenzo Rockito Priori * (105)
"Quesadilla" by Gwen Harlow (106)
"Quince Celebration" by Eneas De Troya *
[http://myspace.com/rockito] (106)
"Mexican Market" by Wonderlane (107)
"Baby Jesus Doll" by Steven Depolo *
[http://flavors.me/stevendepolo] (108)
"Our Lady of Guadalupe Statue" by Andreanna Moya * (109)
"Snow in Guadalajara" by anonymous (110)

ABOUT CULTUREALL & ICIU

"Guitar Lessons" courtesy Sherry Gupta (111)

CREDITS

"Carpathian Shepherd with Donkey" by Falk Kienas (115)
"Production Group Meeting" by Phillip Harder (116)
"Zakery's Bridge Production Group" by Eric Hermann (117)

BACK COVER

"Jenny Reuling" by Phillip Harder

About the Creators

KAY FENTON SMITH (writer)

Kay grew up in central New York surrounded by stories of her ancestors from England and Germany. A childhood friend from Korea also inspired her to seek out friends and stories from around the world, which eventually led to writing Zakery's Bridge. Today she writes and teaches workshops in central Iowa where she lives with her husband, Elliott, and their children, Freddy and Sarah.

CAROL ROH SPAULDING (writer)

Carol Roh Spaulding is the granddaughter of Korean immigrants. A native Californian, she received her doctorate from the University of Iowa and has taught creative writing and American multicultural literature at Drake University since 1996. She writes for both children and adults, and her short fiction has won numerous national literary awards. She lives in Des Moines with her husband, Tim, and their son, Jonah.

JUSTIN NORMAN (designer / photographer)

Justin has been designing for over ten years and currently takes the lead on web and print projects for Shrieking Tree. When not designing, he can be found writing music for Make-Believe Machines, articles for *Hi-Fructose* magazine, or working with a local anti-torture group.

PHILLIP HARDER (photographer)

Phillip Harder is a photographer, writer, and human being. Having obtained a undergraduate degree from Drake University, he is currently a professor of photography at Des Moines Area Community College. He continues to be an active member of Shrieking Tree. In his free time he travels, but not enough.

DANNY HEGGEN (producer)

Danny is a writer and musician. He has penned three books, including one about a women's prison in Australia, *Voices on Inside: the Women of Boronia*, a collection of stories from homeless teenagers, *From a Growing Community, Iowa's Homeless Youth*, and the forthcoming *So If One Thought Thinks of Me*. He writes and performs music with his band, Seedlings, and works for local non-profit, Community!Youth Concepts.

SPECIAL THANKS

Kim & Ted Heggen, Katy Schumacher, Kate Truscello, Tyler Biggs, Ryan Stier, Chris Ford, Dustin Smith, Des Moines Social Club, Amy & Dave Croll, Cheri Doane, Eric Hermann, Cassie Beverly, Amanda Doran, Michael Chilton, Shannon Garcia, Sara Lancaster, Tracey Manson, Tim Bascom, Tanya Keith, Mary Martinez, Joan Fenton Seabrook, everyone who came out to the 2nd Annual Community Bash, Wesley Norman, and everyone else who contributed their time, money, and resources to this book.

* These images were used under a Creative Commons license. Other photos were used with written consent from their authors or purchased. Additional art by Justin Norman.

Thank you for purchasing *Zakery's Bridge*. To find information on related events, schedule a speaking event of your own with the authors, or purchase additional copies of the book, please visit us online at **www.ZakerysBridge.com**.